A TOWPA'
IN OX

The Canal and River Thames between
Wolvercote and the City

MARK J. DAVIES AND CATHERINE ROBINSON

In fond memory of Jack and Rose Skinner,
veterans of the Oxford Canal

Oxford Towpath Press

2012

Image on front cover and title page:
'The Hythe Bridge with Tower of the Castle',
engraved from a drawing by Peter de Wint
for the Oxford University Almanac of 1835.

© Mark J. Davies and Catherine Robinson 2001, 2003, 2012

Second edition 2012

ISBN 978-0-9535593-4-3 2nd edition
(ISBN 0-9535593-1-9 1st edition)

A catalogue record for this book is available from the British Library.

Published by Oxford Towpath Press, c/o Mark J. Davies,
12 Hythe Bridge Arm, Oxford Canal, Oxford OX1 2TA
(tel. 01865 798254).

towpathpress@btopenworld.com
www.oxfordwaterwalks.co.uk

Typeset by Alison Beaumont and Bryony Clark
to an original design by Ruth Bateson, who also did the drawings.

Printed by Berforts Information Press Ltd,
Oxford, UK

Contents

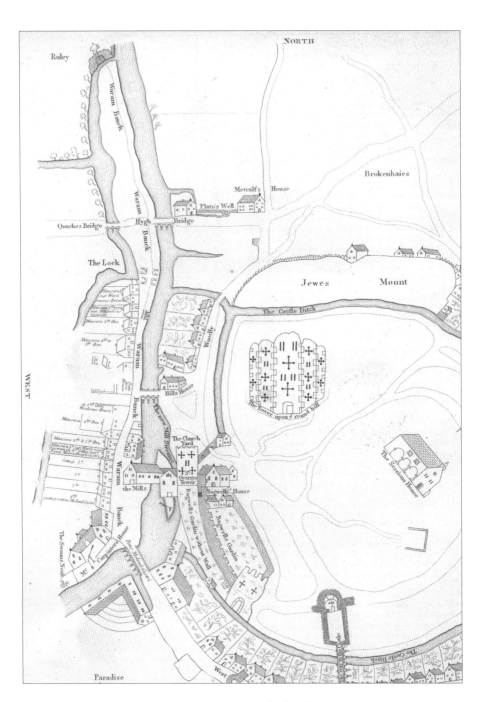

NORTH

Ruley

Waram Banck

Brokenhaies

Metcalf's House

Plato's Well

Quackes Bridge   Hygh Bridge

Waram Banck

The Lock

Jewes   Mount

The Castle Ditch

WEST

Woodly

Hills House

The new Mill Stream

Waram Banck

The Church Yard

The Tower upon y round Hill

St. George's Tower

the Mills

Bagwells House

Bagwells Garden without Wall

The Sessions House

Carpenters House

Bagwells Garden

The Swanns Neck

Mr.

Paradise   West

The Castle Ditch

Preface

When W.M. Wade produced his book *Walks in Oxford* in about 1817, he was surprised that so few guidebooks had been produced about 'a city so abounding in objects of high and commanding interest'. Today Oxford is a city as much written about as any in the world, yet in 1998, when we came to research the predecessor to this book (*Our Canal in Oxford: Along the Towpath from Wolvercote to Jericho and the City*), it became obvious that the Oxford Canal had been accorded only a minimum of attention. Our city of high academic and aesthetic ideals, of dreaming spires and inspired dreamers, has treated the workaday canal as an embarrassment to be tolerated at best, but more usually ignored.

Yet the social impact of the canal on Oxford has been huge, and our first book was an attempt to record the essence of the unique way of life of the working boatpeople before their memories, like the canal carrying trade, were gone for ever. The enthusiastic response to that book included two comments of particular note from other authors. Sheila Stewart, author of *Ramlin' Rose: The Boatwoman's Story*, observed: 'Times change so quickly, it's very important to capture the facts and features while they are still there', and the author and *Guardian* columnist George Monbiot commented: 'I spent a wonderful day walking the route with a party of friends, taking turns to read aloud from *Our Canal in Oxford* as we passed the places it described. The book has made this familiar landscape fascinating to me.'

Our Canal in Oxford inevitably touched on matters relating to the River Thames. Its successor, *A Towpath Walk in Oxford*, first published in 2001 – while repeating, amending, or expanding upon the original text in respect of the canal – covered this more ancient and pastoral of Oxford's waterways in greater detail. A particular theme of this book is the effect on Oxford of the completion of the new Oxford Canal in 1790. In conjunction with the Thames & Severn Canal, which facilitated trade from the west when it joined the Thames at Lechlade in 1789, the Oxford Canal provided an unprecedented impetus for change in a largely

Opposite: Extract from a copy of an early 17th-century map of Oxford Castle, held at Christ Church. Of note is the lasher at 'Ruley', 'Plato's Well', and the Castle Mills next to 'St George's Tower'. Upper and Middle Fisher Rows have yet to appear on the 'Waram Banck'.

timeless city accustomed to centuries of academic seclusion. The 1790s was also a time of great change for Oxford's close-knit communities of river boatmen, many from families who had plied the same unchanging trade for centuries. Some exploited the new opportunities presented by the canal, some foundered in the face of its superior competition, and some adapted to new, often related, activities. Certain names predominate: Bossom, Beesley, Corbey, Crawford, Gardner, Howkins, and Skinner, for instance, and we are indebted to the painstaking work of the late Mary Prior in compiling the family trees of these and other prominent local boating families. On the bank, the names Ward and Tawney stand out.

In this second edition, the third part, relating to the Thames, has been largely rewritten, as too has part of the Jericho section, where the changes over the last decade have been particularly marked. But in Jericho – described by local author Philip Pullman in 2002 as 'having a hidden character, more raffish and jaunty altogether, with an air of horse-trading, minor crime, and a sort of fairground bohemianism' – residents continue staunchly and imaginatively to resist change (with Pullman playing a leading role), taking heart from the successful campaign to defend the Trap Grounds.

Sources

In addition to the oral and archive sources mentioned below, and the publications listed in the bibliography, several unpublished works held at the Bodleian Library have been consulted. Chief among them are the notebooks and collections of Henry Minn (1870–1961), a former Bodleian librarian, whose personal reminiscences of the late 19th century are especially informative. *A Scrapbook of Jericho* by Miss C.L.M. Hawtrey proves the value of oral history, capturing the reminiscences of long-term residents of Jericho who were able in 1956 to cast their minds back to the days when the suburb had only just reached the sodden margins of the canal. Finally, the unpublished notes of the pioneering photographer and historian Henry Taunt (1842–1922), now held at the Oxfordshire History Centre in Cowley, have also proved most revealing.

In addition, we have drawn on the observations of two of Oxford's most famous early historians, Anthony Wood (1632–1695) and Thomas Hearne (1678–1735). Extracts from *Jackson's Oxford Journal*, Oxford's principal newspaper from 1753 onwards, are cited frequently; for ease of reading, the capital letters which were used with all nouns at that time have been have been edited down.

The archives of the Proprietors of the Company of the Oxford Canal Navigation (often referred to in our text as 'the Canal Company', or simply 'the Company'), held at Warwick County Record Office and the Public Record Office in Kew, have provided much previously unpublished material, as have the archives of the Gentlemen Commissioners of the Thames Navigation, held at the Berkshire County Record Office in Reading. Closer to home, parish records and Oxford trade directories were among the most helpful materials held in the Westgate Library in Oxford, the Oxfordshire History Centre in Cowley, and the Bodleian Library.

Acknowledgements

Many people contributed their memories and insights to this book, principally **Jack Skinner and his wife Rose (née Hone)**, whose respective families have a long tradition on the working boats, and who themselves spent most of their working lives afloat before retiring 'to the bank' in 1962. Jack (John Thomas Skinner) was taken on board his parents' boat at Braunston at the age of three weeks in 1919, and spent the rest of his life on or by the water. He could trace his boating ancestry back to the Monk family of Dudley on his mother's side, and on his father's to a boating great-grandfather, Samuel Skinner, born in the Oxfordshire village of North Leigh in about 1798. Rose was descended from the Hones of Banbury, boatmen from at least the 1840s, while her great-grandfather, Richard Hall, was a boatman from Foleshill, Coventry, where Rose was born in 1924. Jack died in 2008, and it was the death of Rose in June 2012 which caused us to revise and republish this book.

We thank all the other contributors to the first edition (many of whom have also passed away, a timely reminder of the importance of capturing personal reminiscences before they are lost for ever): **Michael Stockford**, born at The Plough Inn near the canal in Wolvercote in 1931 ... **Ray Venney**, resident on Wolvercote Green within sight of the water from 1926 … **Jessie Harding,** who lived in Hayfield Road by the canal from 1910 … her neighbour, **Mrs Doris Thicke** … **Sylvia Johnson,** born in a house by the canal in Kingston Road in 1908 and resident there for 93 years … **Fred Hann,** who lived most of his life in Jericho, and occupied Juxon Street Wharf House as a British Waterways employee in the 1960s … **Ted Harris,** who has lived in Combe Road, Jericho since the 1940s … **Denis Wise,** a resident of Jericho since 1955 … **Ray Titcomb** and his sister, **Della James,** who were born and brought up in Upper Fisher Row in the 1940s … Ray's wife, **Jean,** who lived next door – 'Lazy, aren't we!' – and was the daughter of **Kath Tustin,** who married a descendant of one of Oxford's traditional boating families, and whose son **Colin Tustin** is therefore the sole remaining resident of the Row who can claim a blood-line back to its traditional river-barging days … Kath's sister-in-law, **Pat Weller,** the daughter of Aubrey E. Tustin, who ran The Nag's Head in Middle Fisher Row in the 1930s and 1940s … **Nancy Sherratt,** one of the five daughters of the New Road wharfinger, Bernard Robinson, who lived in a Canal Company property by the wharf between 1922 and 1937. (Coincidentally, Nancy's uncle was Thomas Squires, an author whose book on west Oxford is listed in the Bibliography.) … **Charles Gee,** who acquired Medley Manor Farm in the 1950s … **Heather and Peter Lund,** Binsey residents since 1950 … **John Ballance,** owner of Bossom's Boatyard at Medley from 1953, and his son **Tom Ballance.**

Valuable help was also given by British Waterways staff at Braunston and Gloucester, and Nicola Whitewood at Watford in particular; Colin Harris and colleagues at the Bodleian Library; staff at the Centre for Oxfordshire Studies in the Westgate Library in Oxford (now the Oxfordshire History Centre at Cowley); Professor John Barron, Master of St Peter's College; Carl Boardman, County Archivist; Brian Coates; Dr K.F. Hilliard; Paul Hunter for the boat histories on page 50; the late Nick Elwes and Wendy Scanlon; Ann Spokes Symonds; Father Michael Wright; the Magna Gallery, Oxford; and Sanders of Oxford. Hugh Compton, the author of the definitive history of the entire length of the Oxford Canal, read and commented on early drafts and contributed many useful facts and original insights. Caroline

Jackson-Houlston allowed us to use her drawing of a Water Rail on page 13. Ruth Bateson created the original designs for *Our Canal in Oxford*, re-worked by Alison Beaumont and Bryony Clark in the current publication. Thanks are due also to many others, too numerous to mention, for their support and enthusiasm.

Landmarks: a note of caution

The landscape of the Oxford Canal is changing all the time. Since 1998, when we began writing *Our Canal in Oxford*, the predecessor to this book, smart new apartment blocks and town-houses have been built along the west bank of the Castle Mill Stream, and a rash of red-brick luxury developments has spread northwards along the canal, covering much of the land formerly belonging to Lucy's Ironworks and to Unipart. Similar suburbanisation has been the fate of Aristotle Lane. Even Lucy's factory was demolished in 2007, and the future of the last working wharf at Jericho hangs in the balance – and thus the canal's last links with its industrial past have almost all been broken. Despite all these changes, we hope that with the aid of the maps, and the fixed landmarks of the locks and bridges, readers taking real or imaginary journeys along the canal will still be able to visualise how things used to be.

The authors

Mark Davies has lived on a narrowboat in central Oxford since 1992. He is the author of *Stories of Oxford Castle: From Dungeon to Dunghill* (2006), *The Abingdon Waterturnpike Murder: A True-Life Tale of Crime and Punishment* (2008), and *Alice in Waterland: Lewis Carroll and the River Thames in Oxford* (2012). He leads historical and literary walks in Oxford, and gives talks on a range of local history themes (www.oxfordwaterwalks.co.uk).
Catherine Robinson has lived in Hayfield Road, within sight of the canal, since 1982. She is the author (with Liz Wade) of *A Corner of North Oxford: The Community at the Crossroads* (2010), and is the Secretary of the Friends of the Trap Grounds (www.trap-grounds.org.uk).

Mark Johnstone Davies and Catherine Robinson
Oxford, 2001 and 2012

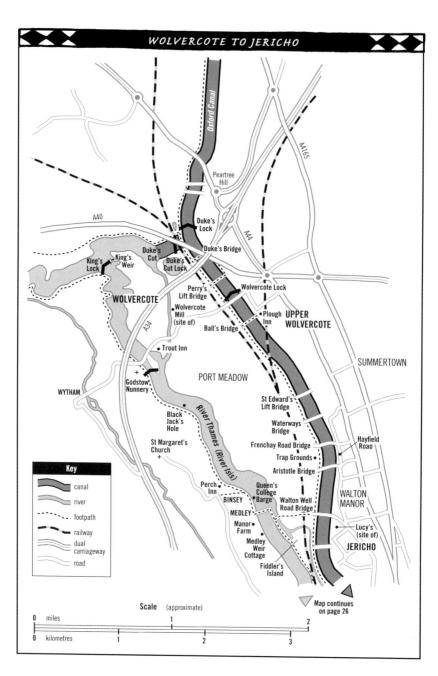

Oxford Canal

Peartree
Hill

A40

A44

A4165

Duke's
Lock

Duke's
Cut

Duke's Bridge

Duke's
Cut Lock

King's
Lock

King's
Weir

Perry's
Lift Bridge

Wolvercote Lock

WOLVERCOTE

Wolvercote
Mill
(site of)

Plough
Inn

UPPER
WOLVERCOTE

Ball's Bridge

A34

Trout Inn

SUMMERTOWN

PORT MEADOW

Godstow
Nunnery

WYTHAM

St Edward's
Lift Bridge

Black
Jack's
Hole

Waterways
Bridge

Hayfield
Road

St Margaret's
Church

Frenchay Road Bridge

Trap Grounds

Aristotle Bridge

Key

canal

river

footpath

railway

dual
carriageway

road

Perch
Inn

Queen's
College
Barge

Walton Well
Road Bridge

WALTON
MANOR

BINSEY

MEDLEY

Manor
Farm

Lucy's
(site of)

JERICHO

Medley
Weir
Cottage

Fiddler's
Island

River Thames (River Isis)

Scale (approximate)

Map continues
on page 26

0 miles 1 2

0 kilometres 1 2 3

◆ x ◆

 The Canal at Wolvercote

It is hard to imagine nowadays, when the Oxford Canal is a quiet backwater of villages and suburbs such as Wolvercote and Jericho, that 200 years ago it was a thriving trade route – one of the most important canals in southern England. Designed by James Brindley, the pioneering canal engineer, and his brother-in-law Samuel Simcock, it was built by the Oxford Canal Navigation Company to provide a link with the Midlands coal-fields.

By the late 18th century, large areas of the upper Thames valley had been cleared of timber, and as a consequence there was a growing demand for coal. Supplies could not be brought by road, the highways being so badly maintained that they were virtually impassable for many months of the year. Coal for Oxford and the surrounding market-towns and villages had to be shipped at great expense in colliers down the east coast of England from Newcastle-upon-Tyne, then loaded into barges at the Port of London and brought up the Thames, which in places was too shallow for easy navigation. When the canal finally reached Oxford from Coventry in 1790, the price of coal fell dramatically and there was great rejoicing. The advent of cheaper supplies gave a kickstart to the local economy, fuelling the operation of the paper mill at Wolvercote, the ironworks and University Press in Jericho, and the many breweries of the town. It was not entirely a coincidence that within 40 years property prices in Oxford had increased fourfold, after a long period of stagnation.

Five feet deep and 16 feet wide, the canal reached Wolvercote in 1788, and a wharf was built on the Green. Coal from Hawkesbury Colliery near Coventry was unloaded here daily. From 1790, market boats passed through Wolvercote twice a week, plying between Oxford and Banbury. Pickford's 'fly boats' (an express service, with frequent changes of horse) carried passengers and parcels between the two towns four times a week. Twice a week, fly boats left Oxford on the six-day journey to Birmingham, and you could even travel on Joule's passenger boat to the Potteries and Merseyside. With all this traffic and trade, Wolvercote Green was a much busier place then than it is now – except, of course, when the canal was frozen over, as it was for twelve weeks in the winter of 1795, when *Jackson's Oxford Journal* noted 'great distress among the Oxford poor from the severity of the weather and the long continuance of the frost'. The price of coal, fetched from Banbury in hand-carts, went up every day, until it had quadrupled. 'At length on the 4th of March, to the joy and comfort of the inhabitants, canal-boats arrived with a supply of coal.'

Duke's Cut

In 1789, half a mile to the north of Wolvercote Green, a private cut was constructed for George, the fourth Duke of Marlborough – a local landowner and a major shareholder in the Oxford Canal Company. (He had made a shrewd investment: by 1792 one original share in the company was being offered for sale in *Jackson's* for 190 guineas – at a time when 44 guineas would have bought you five shares in the Grand Junction Canal.) The Duke's Cut extended westwards for 250 yards, linking the canal with Wolvercote Mill Stream, a backwater of the river Thames. The Cut gave control of traffic between the canal and the river to the Duke, who was always in need of money for the upkeep of Blenheim Palace at Woodstock. It also meant that raw materials could be delivered by boat to his paper mill, which was leased in 1782 to William Jackson, an Oxford printer, bookseller, and stationer who was the proprietor of the journal that bore his name. His business supplied paper for Bibles printed by the expanding Clarendon Press (an imprint of Oxford University Press). The mill benefited in another way from the construction of the Cut, in that its machinery was powered by water, the supply of which – until the alternative route was provided – was often interrupted by the requirements of river boats passing over King's Weir on the Thames.

Wolvercote Mill began burning coal to drive its new steam engines in 1811. In 1856 the Delegates of the Oxford University Press (who had by now taken on the lease of the mill) bought two horse-drawn narrowboats to ply by turns to and from Moira Colliery on the Ashby Canal in Leicestershire – a round trip of

216 miles – bringing 100 tons of coal each week. Delivering coal to the mill was a tricky operation. Because there was no towpath along the river to the mill, the boat had to drift backwards with the current, and after unloading it was shafted back empty to the junction. Meanwhile the horse would have been taken back along the Cut – probably by the boatman's eldest child – to be fed and rested in the stables at Duke's Lock or at the White Hart Inn in Wolvercote village, a distance of more than a mile. It was a wearisome procedure, and the few boatmen who switched to steam-powered boats after 1876, and the greater numbers who converted their boats to run on diesel engines in the 1920s and 1930s, must have welcomed the advances in technology.

Hugh Compton, author of the definitive history of the entire Oxford Canal, has provided a precise description of the complex manoeuvres undertaken at this point by pairs of mechanically powered craft:

> When the boats reached the junction of the Cut with the mill stream, the tow line was detached from the motor boat, while the butty was turned, and the line was then re-affixed to the stern of the butty. The two boats then floated down with the current, with the butty leading under the control of a steerer, and the motor working backwards. On returning empty, the motor boat hauled the butty backwards against the stream to the junction, at which point the butty was turned, before continuing onwards to the stop-lock in the normal way.

His account of this procedure commands our respect for the skills of the boatpeople. The mill continued to receive coal by boat until May 1952, when Stephen Littlemore, one of the last of the self-employed 'Number One' boat-owners on the Oxford Canal, delivered 46 tons on his boats *Hood* and *Grenville*. From then on, the mill was fuelled by oil, until its closure in the mid-1990s.

Bridge 232 (numbered from Longford, near Coventry), an elegant red-brick construction, still spans Duke's Cut. Where the Cut joins the canal, there is a pound lock. It used to have two pairs of gates, to cope with the varying levels of water between the canal and the river, which could rise and fall by as much as

Lock-keeper's cottage a few yards south of Duke's Lock, with Bridge 232 spanning the eastern end of Duke's Cut in the background.

Photo: Mark Davies

two feet. Now the river is maintained at a constant level, and the lock has only one pair of gates.

There was a well at Duke's Lock, where the boats used to take on clean drinking water. But – interviewed at length for this book – Rose and Jack Skinner, who were both born into the canal trade and worked a pair of boats called *Forget-Me-Not* and *Gertrude* in the early years of their marriage in the 1940s, recalled that for washing they boiled water from the canal in a brass kettle on their cabin range.

From Duke's Lock to Wolvercote Lock

South of Duke's Lock there are two wooden drawbridges, built in the typical Oxfordshire style. The impact of the American War of Independence on transatlantic trade meant that the Canal Company had to economise during the construction of the canal from Banbury to Oxford; as a consequence, 38 minor bridges were built of timber, instead of brick or stone, which were reserved for bridges carrying wagons. Numbered 233 and 234, the two drawbridges south of Duke's Lock both connect with a track to the east, variously known as Nicholls' Lane, Joe White's Lane, and the Black Path, which leads to Goose Green. (Joe White, a carrier in the early years of the twentieth century, lived in a now-demolished house north of Goose Green.) Also on the east bank, opposite some now-ruined cottages on the towpath, was Drewett's Landing, where bricks from Kingerlee's brickworks in Five Mile Drive, opened in 1869, were loaded into narrowboats. In the 1930s and 1940s, in a wooden bungalow in the field behind the old landing stage, lived the Black Hat Gang. Believed to be tinkers 'from London way', these eight men dealt in scrap metal and always wore black trilby hats, indoors and out.

On the west bank, just to the south, a brightly painted narrowboat tiller was erected beside the towpath in 1996: a poignant memorial to Sarah Lowe and Finn and Louise – a mother and her children who died on this stretch of the canal in a fire on their narrowboat. There is no memorial to the 11-year-old child whose death was reported by *Jackson's* on 22 May 1790: a boy who 'as he was endeavouring to cross the lock on Goose Green fell into the new canal, where he was drowned before any assistance could be procured to get him out'. Another tragedy occurred four years later, recorded at an inquest into the death of 'John Roberts, a Shepherd, upwards of seventy years of age, who, the preceding evening in attempting to cross the canal at Woolvercott upper lock, unfortunately fell in, and … was quite dead before there was a possibility of getting him out of the water'.

Bridge 235 at Wolvercote Lock is not the original bridge: that was demolished to make way for the present one, which was built to span both the canal and the Great Western Railway. (The GWR was constructed in the late 1840s, despite opposition from the Oxford Canal Company, which correctly surmised that its profits would suffer.) The area around the lock was a favourite playground of village children in the 1930s, according to Michael Stockford, who was born in 1931 at The Plough Inn on Wolvercote Green, where his father Jack was the landlord from 1929 to 1958 (and his grandfather, Herbert, before that). In a channel on the east bank (known in the dialect of Oxfordshire as 'The Lasher'), which takes run-off water to the pound below the lock, the children would paddle and catch fish by hand; that was when they weren't playing in an old Bullnose Morris car abandoned in a field nearby, or talking to Percy Gardiner, who lived in a Romany caravan near the Black Path, earning his living by repairing cricket bats for St Edward's School and the Oxford colleges. Smelling perpetually of the paraffin on which he ran his ancient AJS motorbike, Percy was one of the colourful characters who led marginal lives along the banks of the canal in the days before the second world war. There seems to be less space for individualists and eccentrics in our present-day society – on the bank, at least.

Wolvercote Green

Another favourite playing place for the village children was College Pool, on the east bank opposite the village hall. Known as 'the feeder', this pond collects surface water from the hillside and feeds it into the canal. It eventually filled with rushes and became derelict, but was restored in 1990 by a group of volunteers and officially designated a Site of Special Scientific Interest.

Just to the south of the feeder was 'the boat-turn', a V-shaped opening cut into the eastern bank. Ray Venney, resident on Wolvercote Green since 1926, described to the author how it worked: after delivering coal from the Midlands to Wolvercote Wharf, a short way farther down, a boat would be towed backwards up the canal by the horse, until it was level with the turn; the boatman would manoeuvre his craft until it lay across the canal, and then shaft it into the turn stern-first. The horse then towed the boat out, and the boatman would steer the prow northwards, to begin the return journey. It was opposite the boat-turn, one memorable day in the 1930s, that an eight-year-old boy named Dave Walker caught a pike bigger than himself.

Michael Stockford described how the narrowboats would tie up along the bank near the boat-turn, waiting their turn to go down to the coal wharves of Oxford, three miles south. The boatwomen would light a fire on the bank, boil up water in a tin bath, bring out dolly tubs and mangles, and do the family wash. The men would relax with jugs of ale fetched from The Plough (they never drank in the pub, for some reason). Meanwhile the children from the boats and the boys and girls from the village would play together, paddling and catching tiddlers, collecting bulrushes (which they called 'pokers'), and messing about in a hollow elm tree called The Crocodile, to the south of The

A boatman, possibly from the Howkins family, photographed with his children and horse beside the Oxford Canal, c.1900. Wooden bobbins, often painted bright colours, prevented the traces from chafing the animal's flanks.

Copyright:
Oxfordshire County Council, Oxfordshire History Centre

Plough. Sometimes the local children would be invited on board the boats, which Michael Stockford recalled as spotlessly clean, with shining brasses, gleaming plates, and neat crochet work, and tiers of bunks in the cabin, to sleep as many as eight people. He remembered the canal families as 'very polite'. The captains took great pride in the appearance of their boats, especially those who owned their own vessels. These men (and a few women) were known as 'Number Ones', and there were more of them on the Oxford than on any other canal, because the Company did not own its own fleet of boats.

It would be interesting to know whether the boatchildren ever attended school in Wolvercote on days when their parents were laid up on the canal. Officially, the children were required to attend school and were not permitted to work on the boats before the age of 14. Unofficially, they were expected to help their parents from an early age. Rose Skinner, interviewed for this book, recalled:

'I was about eight when I started doing jobs for my Dad [Alfred Hone Jnr, master of a pair of boats, White City and Rose and Betty]. *I used to steer the boat, standing on a stool, while my sister Bet would walk ahead with the mule and open the lock gates.'*

And did they attend school, as the law required?

'It was a waste of time to go to school just for an hour or two. We used to go sometimes in Longford; three of us at one desk! The teacher would give us a book and say, "Read what you can". Well, if you can't read, how can you read what you can? And then our Mam would come and say, "We're loaded now, you'll have to come away". That's all the schooling we had.'

The boatpeople may not have been literate, but in most of them numeracy was highly developed, and they were extremely skilled in handling boats, horses, engines, and cargoes.

On Sundays, when most locks were closed, some of the boatpeople might have attended a service at St Peter's Church or the Baptist Chapel in Wolvercote. According to Jack Skinner, *'The boatpeople were religious in their own way, but we couldn't read, so we felt daft in church. But my mother always went on Sundays if there was one close by. And she would never throw soap-suds away on a Good Friday.'* (Jack's mother was Ada Skinner, born into the Monk family, aristocrats of the canal who trace their ancestry back to Thomas Monk of Dudley, one of the first canal carriers and boat builders, after whom the traditional narrowboats were named 'monkey boats'.)

Ball's Bridge and The Plough

The Plough Inn on Wolvercote Green dates from at least 1812, when John Ball was the landlord. He died in 1840, aged 74, and bequeathed the pub to his daughters, who sold it. It was rebuilt in 1840, and bought by Morrell's Brewery in 1857. The stables at The Plough were used as a temporary mortuary in cases of drowning during the 19th century.

The children of the boats must have counted themselves lucky if their parents were moored in Wolvercote at the end of August, in the week before St Giles' Fair in Oxford, when Hebborn's Fair came to the Green outside The Plough. There were coconut-shies and hoop-la stalls and the 'galloping horses' carousel owned by Hatwells of Cassington. At quiet times, the man in charge would give the children free rides.

Opposite The Plough on the east bank is Wolvercote Wharf, its stone slabs still in place, but now overgrown with grass and weeds. Ray Venney watched roadstone being unloaded there from a Warwickshire quarry in his childhood; but by 1930 the wharf was used only by Henry Osborne-King, the corn merchant who lived at Church Farm. His wagons would bring hay and straw from Pixey Meadow, to be loaded on to boats and taken to the Midlands. Eventually, however, even these loads were being transported by rail: a sign of the economic decline of the canal system, which had begun with the advent of competition from the railways in the 1840s and accelerated during the first world war, when many boatmen were conscripted into military service.

Immediately south of the wharf stood (and still stands) a brick bridge, number 236, known as Ball's Bridge, which used to lead to a railway crossing. It was over this bridge that the young Michael Stockford would go on his train-spotting expeditions in the 1930s. When a train was waiting on this stretch of line, he would sometimes be sent to fetch threepence-worth of ale from The Plough for the engine driver and stoker, who meanwhile would fry up eggs and bacon on their shovel in the cab.

 ## Wolvercote to Frog Lane

The next bridges south of Wolvercote are 237 (a brick bridge, carrying the railway line to Bicester), and then 238, a wooden drawbridge built in 1831. No track leads to it or away from it, so presumably it was constructed for the benefit of livestock passing over the canal to graze. Although it is known as St Edward's School Bridge, it cannot have been built for the convenience of the boys, because the school was not established on its canal-side site until 1873. One of its early pupils was Kenneth Grahame (1859–1932), who in later life earned immortality as the author of *The Wind in the Willows*. It was probably along this stretch of the Oxford Canal that he first observed horse-drawn narrowboats, one of which found its way eventually into his book:

Round a bend in the canal came plodding a solitary horse,
stooping forward as if in anxious thought. From rope traces
attached to his collar stretched a long line, taut, but dipping with
his stride, the further part of it dripping pearly drops.

Mr Toad watches from the water's edge as the boat approaches:

With a pleasant swirl of quiet water at its blunt brow, the barge
slid up alongside of him, its gaily painted gunwale level with the
towing-path, its sole occupant a big stout woman wearing a linen
sun-bonnet, one brawny arm laid along the tiller.

This fine descriptive passage is only slightly flawed by the author's
misuse of the word 'barge'. It is a common mistake. Barges are
wide and flat, and they work on rivers and wide canals. The vessels
which plied (and still ply) the lesser canals like the Oxford
are called narrowboats. Kenneth Grahame
introduced further confusion by calling
the whiskery hero of his book 'Ratty'.
Ratty, with his blunt snout, round face, and
small neat ears, was not a rat but a water vole,
Arvicola terrestris. It is fitting that along this
stretch of the canal there still lives a community of
these shy creatures, one of only five colonies identified in a
survey of all the waterways in the city of Oxford in 1997.

To the west of the canal at this point is Hook Meadow,
another Site of Special Scientific Interest. Described technically
as 'unimproved neutral meadow', it is a piece of marshy grassland
now rare in the Oxford area. Marsh marigolds grow here, and
ragged robin and meadowsweet; waterfowl such as snipe and jack
snipe are attracted to the site in wintertime. Fred Chamberlain,
in his unpublished memoir, 'Recollections Of Wolvercote As
It Was In 1910', recorded that 'On Port Meadow a budding
aeronaut named Gooden tried out his aeroplane, which local
people called "The Grasshopper", for it hardly ever left the
ground for more than a few yards, and he had his hangars in
Hook Meadow, by the railway.'

'The Radiators'

South of Hook Meadow, on the opposite bank, was once a brick-yard, established around 1850. In one of the clay pits here, in 1871, workmen discovered a complete skeleton of *Eustreptospondylus*. This carnosaur of the Jurassic times – 150 million years ago – is now housed in the University Museum, the most intact specimen in western Europe. The antiquarian scholar, Henry Minn, recording that flooding had rendered the brick-pits unworkable by 1912, recalled Mr Webb, their owner, as 'a well liked man and a prominent member of the North Oxford Sports Club. At their festive meetings it was always endeavoured to get him to sing "Pretty Polly Perkins of Paddington Green" in an interminable number of verses, he swinging a cricket bat in time to the chorus. He became depressed later and was found drowned in one of his pits.'

By 1925 the brick-yard had closed down to make way for William Morris's Osberton Radiators Factory, which moved here from Osberton Road in Summertown. The factory made radiator grilles for the 'Bullnose Morris' automobile, and during the second world war it made radiators for the engines in Spitfire, Lancaster, Halifax, and Mosquito bombers. Three thousand people were employed on the site during the war, and the factory continued to work flat out in peace-time, making parts for the Morris 8 and Morris Minor cars. The factory sites on both banks of the canal were linked in 1930 by the construction of bridge 239A, the only electrically powered lift bridge on the Oxford Canal (demolished in 2001 after the construction of a fixed bridge, faced with brick, giving access to the new Waterways estate).

Jack and Rose Skinner regularly delivered coal to 'The Radiators' from Bedworth and Griff collieries on the Ashby Canal near Coventry. In the 1940s, Barlow's, the carrying company, paid them 3/9d per ton, which amounted to about £6 for a full load. The round trip took two weeks, and they were not paid for the week in which they returned empty. (Jack: '*It was a hard life. We used to work 16 or 17 hours a day, six or seven days a week. Many's the time me and her have set off before dawn and finished in the dark.*' … Rose: '*We used to eat as we went along – and I used to cook as we went along an' all! Cooking with one hand and steering with the other. And the little ones* [they had four children] *playing in the empty hold, or tied to the chimney when we were loaded.'*) Although coal was their staple cargo, the Skinners also carried timber and tar. During the last war Jack even transported a top-priority consignment of nitro-glycerine, which he and his mate delivered from Brentford to Birmingham up the Grand Union Canal, through 153 locks. (*'We did it in 63 hours, without stopping – kept going through the night, with a paraffin lamp on the front of the boat. That put years on me, that did! When we got to the other end, there were chaps all dressed in green fireproof stuff, with gloves and helmets. They said there was enough in one of those bottles to blow up Birnigum with!'*)

We live in a different world from that in which Jack and Rose plied their arduous trade. 'The Radiators' factory has long since gone, like its replacement, that of Oxford Automotive Components. Now the factory on the east bank and the derelict warehouses on the west bank have been replaced by luxury houses and apartment blocks. Ironically, post-industrial 'brownfield' sites are often rich in wildlife, with greater biological diversity than 'greenfield' sites. When the new red-brick villas began to tame and suburbanise the wilderness on the west bank in 2001, some anonymous graffiti scrawled nearby recorded one local person's sense of loss:

> A little piece of Legoland
> will set you back three hundred grand;
> but lizards lost, and vanished vole,
> will halve the value of your soul.

Frog Lane

Turn right off the towpath beyond the Frenchay Road bridge for a short optional detour along Frog Lane and back.

A new brick bridge spans the canal at the end of Frenchay Road. It replaced a heavy metal drawbridge, numbered 239, which was constructed around 1900 and demolished in 2000. Generations of local children tested their strength against the old bridge, and some time before the first world war one of the ten Chappell children from nearby Hayfield Road was killed while operating it or larking about near it. Originally a wooden drawbridge had been constructed here, to carry an ancient right of way which has had several names during the course of its history. In medieval times it was known as 'Wycroft Lane', leading as it did to 'Wythorpte' – later 'Wycroft Close' – a three-acre property near Port Meadow which in 1266 consisted of Wyke Meadow, a 'mansion', and an osier bed. Later the lane became known as 'My Lady's Way' (a probable reference to the abbesses of Godstow, who owned much of the land hereabouts for several hundred years). In the 17th and 18th centuries the lane was known as 'the upper road to Wolvercote'. Some time later it acquired the name Frog Lane, by which it is still known today.

Frog Lane leads due west along the northern edge of the Trap Grounds reed bed, designated as a Local Wildlife Site. This is Oxford's only known breeding site for the Water Rail (*Rallus aquaticus*), illustrated here – an elusive aquatic bird less often seen than heard: when disturbed, it gives vent to a series of grunts, yelps, and squeals, known to ornithologists as 'sharming'. The reed bed is also host to the largest colony of breeding reed warblers in the city, and the county's only recorded population of the spider *Nesticus cellulanus*. Foxes saunter along Frog Lane in broad daylight, and muntjac deer may be glimpsed here in the twilight of summer evenings. Overhead in the big willows, tree-creepers and woodpeckers make their nests in spring.

An area of woodland and scrubland beyond the reed bed was saved from development in 2006 when a long campaign to register the site as a Town Green ended in success in the House of Lords. If this wilderness had disappeared under tarmac, seven species of warbler would have lost their breeding ground, as would a rare colony of viviparous lizards, not to mention grass-snakes, glow-worms, and slow-worms. But their survival is now assured, and the right of local people to wander around the Trap Grounds – enjoying solitude, picking blackberries, observing wildlife – is established in perpetuity.

The name 'Trap Grounds' (in use since at least 1781, when *Jackson's Oxford Journal* announced the auction of 'a Leashold Estate in the Parish of Wolvercott, called the Trap Grounds') was once applied to a much more extensive area on the east side of Port Meadow, beyond the land now occupied by allotments and the Burgess Field nature reserve. The name may be a corruption of the designation 'Extra Parochial', which denoted exemption from the payment of church tithes; or it may record the practice of trapping fish and eels in channels when the river flooded across the Meadow. We shall probably never know.

Returning to the canal along Frog Lane, one might spare a thought for 'Little Mush', a solitary man who lived here in a shed in the 1930s. Isolated from the world by a severe speech impediment, he had a rifle and a spiteful goose (*'to ward off the Social'*, according to local people who remember him). He used to pick coals from the railway line, and was always filthy. (*'Once his sister persuaded him to go and live with her in Reading, but she made him have a bath, so he came back the next day.'*) In an old hen-coop somewhere in this vicinity lived 'Paraffin Liz', reputed once to have been the Librarian of Somerville College. In the 1920s and 1930s she made a living by giving riding lessons to children on Port Meadow (allegedly using horses that did not belong to her). According to local legend, *'she always rode bare-back. She was a queer old soul, as skinny as a herring. She wore men's boots, and string for a belt, and her niece paid for her to have dinner in the Randolph Hotel every night.'*

At the entrance to Frog Lane, near the towpath, is a crescent-shaped pond, created in 2000 to provide an alternative habitat for the water voles and water rails and other creatures under threat of eviction by the new housing developments in the area. The pond project was the result of a collaboration between the City Council, which now owns the Trap Grounds, and local volunteers who have cleared tons of rubbish from the scrubland, created new paths, and removed invasive scrub willows from the Reed Bed.

Opposite the end of Frog Lane there used to be a small wharf, where the electricity sub-station is now. Known as Hambridge's Wharf (although it was leased by the Corporation of Oxford from 1900 to 1925), it sold coal and firewood to local householders. Many generations of the extensive Hambridge family, originally from Banbury, were connected with the canal as boatmen and coal merchants, from its very beginnings in the 18th century.

Hayfield Wharf

South of the sub-station on the east bank are the long, neat gardens of the householders in Hayfield Road (who used to have to pay one shilling each to the Canal Company as annual rent for the use of the bank). Before these houses were built in 1886, there were some cottages, home in the 1840s to a small community of boat-builders, among whom were John Pebody and his wife Ann, with their sons Oliver and Caleb. The Pebody family was well known along the whole length of the Oxford Canal, from Braunston and Banbury down to Oxford. A map of 1846, drawn by a surveyor of the proposed London, Oxford, and Cheltenham Railway, shows a small boat-building dock half-way along the lane that is now Hayfield Road, with a row of dwellings nearby. The registers of St Giles' Parish reveal a shifting population living in the canal-side cottages, with a high rate of infant mortality. Henry Minn, recalling his childhood in the 1870s, described the cottages as squalid, and the lane as muddy. He recalled that the inhabitants made a living from selling faggots. Conditions improved greatly in the late 1880s, when the Oxford Industrial and Provident Land and Building Society laid out the modern roadway and built a street of 'model artisans' cottages … sound and healthy dwellings, to let at moderate rents'.

The canal has always played a large part in the lives of the Hayfield Road community. Until the 1950s it was clean enough for the children to swim in, and Mrs Jessie Harding, born in 1910 and resident in the street all her life, remembered in her ninetieth year: *'You could see the bottom from the drawbridge to Aristotle Lane, and it was full of roach and perch. We used to fish for "red soldiers"* [perch?] *with a bent pin and a bit of string.'* The late Mrs Doris Thicke, another long-time resident, recalled:

'The canal people were very friendly. The same families would travel up and down the canal all year. I remember the Skinners and the Beauchamps. They all waved when they passed the end of our garden. The men used to throw their boots into the garden of number 3, for Tommy Tombs to mend them. They would collect them on the way back up. The boats had glistening brasses, and

clothes hung out to dry, as white as milk. Those women were tough! They wore hob-nailed boots, and unloaded coal just like the men. But they put on clean aprons and caps to visit Dolly's Hut [The Anchor Inn in Hayfield Road, opposite the wharf]. *They couldn't read or write: they just signed with a cross.'*

Rose Skinner (wielding the shovel) and Jean Humphries (holding the barrow steady), unloading coal at Juxon Street Wharf in Jericho, 1956.

Copyright: Oxfordshire County Council, Oxfordshire History Centre

The Anchor was originally a hostelry known as Heyfield's Hutt, named after William Heyfield, the landlord who presided over it from at least 1721 and died there at the age of 90 in 1778. In his time, the inn seems to have been a haunt of card-sharps. We learn from *Jackson's Oxford Journal* (25 February 1764) of a game of cards there in which the eminent Dr Webb, a tooth-drawer, blood-letter, and wig-maker, lost 44 guineas and the mortgage deeds of two houses in the parish of St Thomas. Never the most reputable of hostelries, the inn was frequented in the 19th century, according to Henry Minn, by undergraduates who brought their dogs for the purposes of rat-coursing in the neighbouring fields and on Port Meadow, 'a bag of rats being supplied by local waterside loafers'.

Longevity was the hallmark of the landlords of the inn: Anthony Harris took over the licence in 1796 and died 51 years later, still presiding over the bar, in 1847. Although the inn was renamed as The Anchor in the 1840s and rebuilt in the 1930s, it was universally known until quite recently as Dolly's Hut, taking the name from another landlord, William Dolley, who kept the house for a quarter of a century from 1852. The pub was a favourite with boatpeople, and it is tempting to imagine Rose Skinner's grandfather, Alfred Hone senior, singing in the snug in the 1890s:

'He could play the squeezebox, and dance and sing, all at the same time. He had a clear true whistle too, and a rattle of wooden bobbins. "Shake them bobbins!" he used to sing. It was a song the old boat-chaps used to sing to make their 'orses get a move on.'

(These recollections of Alfred Hone were recorded by Sheila Stewart in her richly informative book *Ramlin Rose: The Boatwoman's Story*.)

Hayfield Wharf was an important feature of the Oxford Canal from its earliest days. *Jackson's* recorded on 3 October 1789:

The Oxford Canal being finished and opened at the wharf at Hayfields Hutt, within a quarter of a mile of Oxford, the best coals are sold at the following prices: Oakthorpe coals, 1s 5d. per cwt; Warwickshire 1s 2d per cwt; Staffordshire coke per ton, £1 4s. 9d.

Coal merchants came long distances with horse-drawn carts to take deliveries from the wharf. Trade was so brisk that within six months of the opening of the wharf the minute book of the Oxford Canal Company recorded an instruction to the Company's contractors to 'repair forthwith the Carriage Road [Rackham's Lane, now St Margaret's Road] from the Turnpike Road [Woodstock Road] to Hayfield Hutt'.

Although the Company was keen to be a good neighbour, not everyone, it seemed, welcomed the advent of the canal. On 12 December 1789, *Jackson's* carried a notice denouncing 'some evil-minded Person or Persons' who on the previous Sunday night had 'feloniously and maliciously' removed several hatch gates from the towing path leading from Heyfield's Hutt to Woolvercot, thrown them into the water, and done other damage to the works of the canal. A reward of £5 was offered for information, with the warning that the crime carried a penalty of transportation for seven years. This was not an isolated act of sabotage: in June 1791, five towpath gates were broken down. Evidently vandalism is not an exclusively modern problem – and nor is the use of the towpath

as a thoroughfare: anyone riding along it, the Company sternly pronounced in 1791, would be prosecuted 'with the utmost rigour'.

Besides serving as a distribution point for coal (and probably other goods such as slate, salt, and road-stone), Hayfield Wharf was the site of considerable industrial activity. The first known reference to a boat-repair yard here appears in *Jackson's* on 20 February 1802, followed on 25 April 1812 by a notice announcing the auction of 'a capital dock for boat building'. When St John's College (which had been buying up canal-side plots since the turn of the century) advertised a lease on the wharf to interested parties in 1839, the notice listed the following features, in addition to a dwelling house and four tenements: a covered dock, workshops, sheds, and kilns for the making of bricks, lime, and tiles. At least one brick kiln survived until 1866. There was a weighing office on the wharf, with stables for the boatmen's horses and mules, and more stables in the yard on the south side of Aristotle Bridge. Across the road next to the inn, on the site of the modern Aladdin Garage, were more stables for hire (rendered 'very commodious' in 1788 by one John Bridges, with an eye to the betting fraternity who ran horses in the Oxford Races held annually on Port Meadow).

A boathouse erected in 1790 to the south of the bridge harboured the Canal Company's own boat.

On Hayfield's Hut wharf in the 1870s there was a mission room, which was supported by the congregation of the church of St Philip and St James in Woodstock Road. Sunday afternoon services were held here for the benefit of the boatpeople (for whose welfare and morals there was much concern in Victorian society). The Women's Guild of the church paid half the rent, and several of the men from this prosperous, philanthropic congregation taught at a night school held there during the winter months. The mission room was pulled down in 1883.

Some time around 1875, a tall brick building called The Navigation Arms was built on the wharf. Here lived Thomas Johnson, described in the Oxford Directory as a 'coal and manure merchant and beer retailer'. He was assisted by his son-in-law, Anthony Harris (son of the landlord of The Anchor on the opposite side of the road). On wash-days in the 1920s, Mrs Mary Harris, wife of Albert Harris, the foreman on the wharf, would cook faggots and peas on her kitchen range, and the women of Hayfield Road would send their children down the street with basins to fetch dinner for the family. Local boys could earn a few pence by helping to groom and feed the boatmen's horses after school. The wharf closed down in the early 1950s, but Navigation House lingered on until the 1960s, when it was demolished to make way for the offices of Midland Builders (and latterly Oxford Designers and Illustrators).

A familiar feature of the wharf in our own times is the narrowboat *Venturer*, which is moored here when not cruising on the waterways with parties of disabled people, elderly people, or children and young people with special needs. Seventy feet long and designed to accommodate wheelchairs, *Venturer* was launched in 1988 by the Prince of Wales. The scheme is managed by the Oxfordshire Narrowboat Trust and run entirely by volunteers.

Opposite:
Opposite: Heyfield Wharf, c.1890, by Henry Taunt. The 1891 census suggests the following identifications (from right): Frank Restall, the owner; Jane Johnson and her husband Thomas, coal merchant, who lived on the wharf in Navigation House (which is out of the picture); and their maid Sarah Simmonds. The two boys in the centre are probably Ernest and Leonard Tuffrey, also living at Navigation House. The well-scrubbed narrowboats appear to be crewed by one man and five women. Note their traditional bonnets and spotless aprons.

Aristotle Lane to Walton Well

The hump-backed brick bridge at Hayfield Wharf is a Grade II Listed Building, built to an original design by James Brindley, the engineer responsible for the canal. It carries an ancient right of way to Port Meadow, known originally as 'the lower way to Wolvercote' (according to Leonard Hutten's *Dissertation on the Antiquities of Oxford* of 1625). Until 1841, when a bridge was built over Walton Well Ford nearer to the city, Aristotle Lane (as the track came to be known) was the chief entrance to the Meadow from the east. Its use was much disputed in the Middle Ages by the city authorities and the Abbesses of Godstow, who owned the surrounding land. Eventually, to keep an eye on the lane and prevent its being blocked, the City built a house at the eastern end, to accommodate 'the reeve's man'. The *Victoria County History* records the presence of a herdsman's house at the gate to the Lane in 1582; it was used in 1603 and 1608 to isolate victims of the plague, and finally fell down in 1629.

On 3 June 1644, King Charles I slipped out of Oxford by night, marching north with 5000 men up the line of what is now Kingston Road, under the shadow of the tree-crowned gravel bank which (according to Hubert Hurst's 1899 *Oxford Topography*) in those days ran along its length. They escaped along Aristotle Lane, to cross Port Meadow, ford the river, and make a dash for the West Country.

The lane acquired its name from Aristotle's Well, sited in what is now the cellar of the house on the corner of Kingston Road (where stood the house of the Norman knight Sir Brooman le Riche in the twelfth century). The 17th-century diarist Anthony Wood recorded that in his day the well was a favourite haunt of scholars, walking out from Oxford in summer (perhaps from Plato's Well, at the bottom of Walton Street?). In 1718 Thomas Hearne noted in his journal that there was a house of refreshment near the well, and it is tempting to suppose that he meant the cottage on the site of the present Anchor Inn which appears on Benjamin Cole's map of Port Meadow, published in 1720. The well, which was fed by a spring, was known in the 19th century as The Wishing Well, or Dolley's Well. When it was bricked up in 1889, according to Henry Minn, the spring burst out and flowed down to the canal through the garden of the end house in Kingston Road. For a short time it was used to make a watercress bed; later the spring-water was conveyed into the canal by a pipe which can still be seen, emerging from the bank just south of Aristotle Bridge.

It was over Aristotle Bridge between 1849 and 1852 that thousands of tons of gravel were taken by tramway from Cabbage Hill (later to become Kingston Road) and Lark Hill (later to become Chalfont Road). The gravel was used for the construction of the Great Western Railway, which was built parallel to the canal, about 200 yards to the west. The removal of the gravel bank cleared the way for the eventual development of this area of north Oxford. Today the only surviving remnant of the bank forms the western boundary of St Margaret's churchyard in Kingston Road. (According to Henry Minn, describing The Anchor Inn as it was in his childhood in the 1870s, the bank had been so high that a door at the back of the inn, 'now opening from one of the upper rooms, had at one time been at ground level'.)

It was under Aristotle Bridge that the Skinners' boat *Redshank*, towing the butty *Greenshank*, got stuck in 1954 or 1955. By the mid-1950s the canal, which had been losing trade to the road hauliers since the war, was no longer being dredged every Whit Monday and was silting up and becoming choked with weeds. There was talk of closing it. Public opposition to the closure was demonstrated at a protest meeting held in Oxford Town Hall on 3 June 1955, chaired by none other than the poet John Betjeman. By this time, Jack and Rose were working for Willow Wren, a small independent carrying company formed in 1953 with some surplus boats bought from British Waterways. Long afterwards, Jack recalled the epic journey that he and Rose undertook, to prove that the canal was still navigable:

> 'Me and her and Willow Wren put our heads together and decided the best way to save the canal was to prove that it could still carry traffic. So we brought 50 tons of coal from Nuneaton to Juxon's wharf for Morrell's Brewery. We did all right till we got to Dolly's Hut. The water there was very shallow, because the kids had thrown rubbish into it. We had to bowhaul the butty through [drag it along with a rope from the towpath], but we did it!'

In 1967 Jack saved the canal from closure a second time. Treasury officials recommended closing it down and filling it in, on the grounds that it was no longer commercially viable. Jack was asked to accompany Barbara Castle, the Minister of Transport, on a

Here there is an option to turn right along Aristotle Lane to PortMeadow, crossing diagonally left to reach the Thames at Medley bridge. (See page 84.)

fact-finding trip along a stretch farther north, near Thrupp. He took the precaution of going out the night before and opening all the sluices, to give the impression that there was more water in the near-derelict canal than there actually was. '*She never knew the difference – and it done the trick*', he recalled with pride many years later. Mrs Castle decided to save the canal, and ultimately secured enough subsidy to keep open 1400 miles of commercially non-viable canals for pleasure cruising. Everyone who now enjoys fishing in the Oxford Canal, or cruising on it, or walking along the towpath should remember with gratitude Jack Skinner and the trick he played on the Minister of Transport.

Bridge 241, 'The Workhouse Bridge', seen from the south: a drawing by Jenny Modéer, based on a photograph of 1868 in the Bodleian Library. The sloping fields on the right are now the gardens of Kingston Road and Southmoor Road. Aristotle Bridge is seen in the background.

The missing bridge

Sharp-eyed walkers along the towpath will have noticed that Aristotle Bridge is numbered 240, and the next bridge south, at Walton Well Road, is number 242. What happened to 241? It is there in the report of the Chain Survey undertaken by the Oxford Canal Company in 1840 (which recorded every bridge, lock, and other notable structure along the 77-mile length of the canal). Ten chains (one-eighth of a mile) from 'Hayfields Hut Bridge' was 'the Workhouse Bridge': just south of where the builder's yard of Hutchins and Green in Southmoor Road (established in 1878) now fronts the canal on the east bank. A photograph taken in 1868 shows it as a timber drawbridge, similar in design to the bridge near St Edward's School. The 1876 Ordnance Survey map shows it clearly, but it was demolished by 1882, when the houses at the north end of Southmoor Road began to be built.

The name 'Workhouse Bridge' links it with the City Workhouse, established on Rats and Mice Hill (now Wellington Square) in 1771. According to the *Victoria County History*, for many years until 1865 the Oxford Board of Guardians, responsible for the welfare of the workhouse inmates, managed a small mixed farm on the banks of the canal, on land known as Pepper Hills. The 1846 map commissioned by the London, Oxford, and Cheltenham Railway shows 'Pepper Hill' on the west bank, and 'Further Pepper Hill' on the east bank, where now the gardens of Southmoor Road slope down to the water. Linking them was Bridge 241, 'the Workhouse Bridge'. This area was sufficiently isolated from the city for a cholera hospital and dispensary to be erected on Further Pepper Hill, after the Radcliffe Infirmary refused to admit victims during the terrible 22-week epidemic of 1832. The location was somewhat ironic, given the popular belief at the time that cholera was spread from town to town by canal boats and their crews. According to Henry Minn, the cholera hospital was later dismantled and re-erected on the west side of Woodstock Road, to serve as an isolation hospital for victims of smallpox; the Ordnance Survey map of 1876 shows a 'Pest House' standing in orchards on land between Polstead and Frenchay roads.

Such harsh realities were not in the mind of the poet James Elroy Flecker, who may have been thinking of this stretch of

'View of the Cholera Hospital, with the Dispensary adjoining erected & fitted up on the Pepper Hills near the Oxford Canal.' c.1835.

Copyright: Oxfordshire County Council, Oxfordshire History Centre

water when he composed his poem 'Oxford Canal' in the early years of the twentieth century:

> When you have wearied of the valiant spires of this County Town …
> Of its red motors and lumbering trams, and self-sufficient people,
> I will take you walking with me to a place you have not seen –
> Half town and half country – the land of the Canal …

'Half town and half country' describes it very well. An Oxford guidebook, published by Ward, Lock & Co. in 1898, describes the canal as presenting 'an arcadian scene of pastoral beauty'. Mrs Sylvia Johnson, who was born in Kingston Road, alongside the canal, in 1908 and lived there for 93 years, remembered this stretch of the canal as far more rural than it is now: '*There was much more wildlife in the old days – water voles, grass-snakes, and dab-chicks. I saw an otter in the Isis from Port Meadow once, and you could hear bitterns by the river.*' Mrs Johnson, interviewed by the author in 1999, recalled that the canal seemed to freeze more often in the old days. She remembered skating to work in the town centre, and the arrival of an iron boat drawn by six horses, carrying eight men on each side, rocking the boat from side to side to break the ice.

Lucy's Ironworks

The semi-rural stretch of water at the back of Kingston and Southmoor Roads ends abruptly under bridge 242, which carries Walton Well Road to Port Meadow. Beyond it on the east bank stood until 2007 the soot-blackened frontage of the factory known as Lucy's – a stark reminder of the industrial origins of the canal system. The firm was founded by William Carter, who in 1812 was trading in Oxford's High Street as an 'ironmonger, hardwareman, brazier, and tinplate worker'. Until 1820 he was in partnership with John Edwards, whose daughter Martha married Thomas Combe of the Oxford University Press (see the next section).

In 1825 Carter moved his foundry to Walton Well from Summertown, north of Oxford. Boatbuilding was already being undertaken here – but evidently so too was metalworking: a William Ward was identified as 'a smith at Walton Well Dock' when his son was baptised at St Giles' Church in 1823. The earliest definitive evidence of the boatyard is an auction notice in *Jackson's* of

Here there is an option to turn right along Walton Well Road to Port Meadow, crossing straight ahead to the Thames at Medley. (See page 84.)

15 May 1819 for 'a piece of ground called The Dock Yard, adjoining Walton Farm, Jericho, in the occupation of Mr Henry Ward' (who is of unknown relationship to William), but by implication it was probably operating from 1812 or soon after. It is tempting to speculate that Ward produced iron boats, in keeping with the thinking of Richard Tawney, the Company's agent and engineer, who wrote in a letter of 20 July 1811: 'I have recommended to the Oxford Canal Company to make their boats in future of iron, and by way of experiment I wish to put an ice boat immediately on the stocks'. Indeed, the Company had ordered its contractors to plate all of their boats with iron as early as 1789.

Carter concentrated on agricultural tools, iron railings, man-hole covers, and lamp-posts (still to be seen gracing many streets in Oxford). His foundry acquired the name 'Eagle' under his successor, Charles Grafton, in 1830; William Lucy took over the firm in the 1860s, and until 2001 it still thrived under his name. The boatbuilding operation, under Henry Ward's son, William, continued to operate until the 1880s. An article in *The Clarendonian* magazine of 1923, recalling Walton Manor in the 1860s, describes a now-vanished scene on the east bank.

> … a Dock, parallel with the Canal, and covered in by a roof on wooden supports, but open at the sides; here boats were both built and repaired. The road to Port Meadow led over the canal by a drawbridge, and over the two railway lines by a level crossing.

There is now no trace of the boatyard; the drawbridge was replaced by a heavy, graceless brick bridge in 1881, and the level crossing was superseded by an iron railway bridge, uncompromising in its ugliness. Few people now remember the ink works, the varnish factory, and the tallow factory which stood on the east bank south of Lucy's. (According to Miss Hawtrey's 1956 *Scrapbook of Jericho*, the tallow factory which stood at the end of Canal Street until about 1912 'smelt to high heaven! The small boys liked it because you could get lots of maggots there with which to fish, but no one else did.') Now even the ironworks itself, which had loomed over the water for nearly 200 years, has disappeared, to be replaced by penthouse apartments and smart town houses. The last link with the canal's industrial past has been broken.

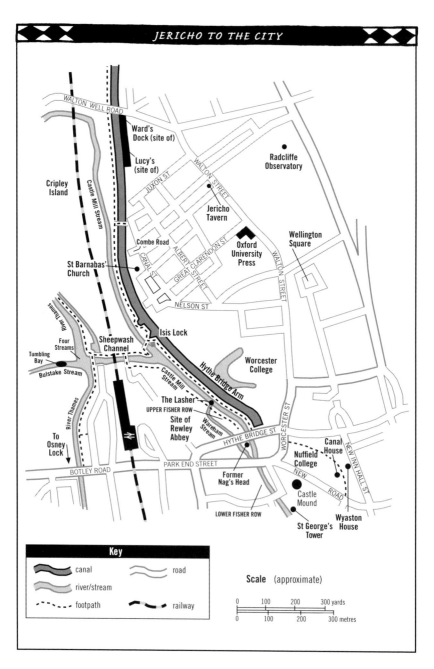

Key

canal	road
river/stream	
footpath	railway

Scale (approximate)

0	100	200	300 yards
0	100	200	300 metres

 Jericho

As the canal approaches Jericho, its character changes a little. Here, in Oxford's first planned suburb, we get the strongest reminders of the canal's true purpose: the movement of boats and the means to load, unload, and service them. A footbridge leads across the canal to Mount Place, the site of the former tallow factory. Next to it was Juxon Street Wharf, the most northerly of a series of wharves stretching down to Worcester College. A wharf house here was occupied by the builders' merchants Stephenson and Co. until the 1920s, when the Canal Company repossessed it as part of a strategic withdrawal from the city centre. Forty years later the wharf played its part in proving the canal's future viability, this being where the British Waterways Board based an experimental hire fleet in the 1960s, when the days of the working boats were clearly finished. Fred Hann, a long-term resident of Jericho, lived in the wharf house there as a BWB employee. As well as setting up the holiday hire fleet, he supervised the running of *Water Rambler*, a purpose-built passenger boat designed to appeal mainly to American tourists, hence a schedule which included Sulgrave Manor (the birthplace of George Washington) on a route through Banbury to Stratford. Started in 1957, it was an ambitious attempt to replicate in miniature the appeal of an ocean-going cruise-liner, with a skipper and hostess in full uniform – although the nights were spent in pre-booked hotel accommodation, not on board. It was *Water Rambler* on which Barbara Castle was taken, when Minister of Transport, to demonstrate the canals' potential for tourism. Juxon Street Wharf was also still a busy coal wharf during Fred's time:

> *'Boats would draw up alongside; the men would shovel the coal from the boat into wheelbarrows, and the women would push them across the yard to create a pile. As it got higher, they'd lay a plank down so they could take a run at it and get the heavy barrow to the top. It was exhausting, dirty work, but somehow they always managed to keep themselves looking tidy.'*

Almost all of this coal was destined for Morrell's brewery in St Thomas' parish, and was collected by horse and cart on a regular basis. *'Of course, lots of coal used to spill into the canal, so I used to rake it all out later. That way I never ever had to buy any coal for myself.'* The boaters also collected letters at the wharf house, and one of Fred's most satisfying tasks was to read out their contents, and write any replies that were needed.

The wharf house was still listed as 'British Waterways (embarkation office)' in Kelly's Directory of 1971, but was replaced by the flats of Castle Mill House the following year. The footbridge was erected at the same time. Both are symbolic. For most of its history, the canal has been a barrier to Jericho, rather than a part of it. The flats here represented a breakthrough, the first opportunity since the inception of the suburb in the 1830s for Jericho to claim a stake in the waterway which defined its western edge.

The land through which the Jericho section of canal was dug in 1789 was known as Little and Great Bear Meadows. The name must derive from the Bear Inn (in central Oxford), the licensee Thomas Furse, a 'singing man' of Christ Church, having acquired the land in 1571. By the 1780s, the Meadows were in the possession of the Reverend Peter Wellington Furse, living in Devon, to whom the Canal Company paid £295 13s, plus eight years' backdated rent, in 1798. In July 1825, Furse sold the plot on which the Oxford University Press was to be built, and soon after relinquished the adjacent fields for Jericho's first houses. Finally he auctioned the remaining 14 acres of Little and Great Bear Meadows (which lay more or less to the west of today's Albert Street) in 1827. Earlier, these fields had been leased to John Stephens, almost certainly a relative of the man of the same name whom the historian Anthony Wood met at 'Jericho Gardens' (the public house-cum-farm on Walton Street) on 1 July 1668, this being the earliest known reference to the name 'Jericho'. The coalmerchant Henry Ward (c.1781–1852), with his dock already established at Walton Well, purchased a large plot close to Worcester College at the southern end of Great Bear Meadow, and went on to establish a wharf there (see page 35). When Ward made his will in 1844 (proved in 1852), he owned some 15 acres of land in Jericho, eight of which he had purchased from Furse.

Opposite:
'The Observatory and Printing Office' c.1850 by Carl Rundt from *A Walk Round Oxford*. This idealised view across the Bear Meadows is unusual both because of its inclusion of the canal and for its depiction of that rare Oxford thing: industrial enterprise! The Oxford University Press building was completed in 1832. Jericho House (subsequently the Jericho Tavern) is shown in the centre.

It took six decades for the open fields to be transformed into the narrow streets of compact houses which in essence still distinguish the Jericho of today. The Bear Meadows resisted development longest, due to their waterlogged nature, and Robert Hoggar's detailed map shows that building had reached only as far as today's Albert Street by 1850. One significant feature was a track running from Henry Ward's wharf, between garden plots parallel to Worcester College's wall, in the direction of the Oxford University Press. It seems likely that construction materials for the new printing works might have arrived by canal and been moved along this track, though as the entire operation was contracted to a London builder, the details of the logistics are unlikely ever to be known.

Difficulties of sanitation were another deterrent to growth, and in 1848 Dr W.P. Ormerod described in *Sanitary Condition of Oxford* 'a drain of the filthiest kind' running 'quite open to the end of Nelson Street' – to exactly the point at which the track from Ward's wharf encountered the first houses, in fact. In her 1956 *Scrapbook of Jericho,* Miss C.L.M. Hawtrey recorded the persistent tradition (incorporated into R.D. Blackmore's *Cripps, the Carrier,* set in 1838) that the part of Jericho next to the canal was 'first a marsh and refuge of footpads and then to all intents and purposes a slum, through which policemen preferred to walk in couples'.

With improved sanitation and building techniques, residential Jericho edged closer to the canal, and Canal Street was laid out in about 1860. For the first time, canal boatmen and Jericho residents came face to face on a regular basis. Miss Hawtrey noted a comment from the notebook which Richard Gillett, a Canal Company engineer, used to keep on board the Company inspection launch, *The Lady Godiva.* In 1865 he observed that in Jericho the boatmen 'had the reputation of being extremely illiterate and very much addicted to a beer which went by the name of "Fourpenny" and was extremely intoxicating'.

If some of Jericho's residents were wary of the boatmen, outsiders continued to fear Jericho itself, as this example from the *Scrapbook* shows. As a boy, Montague Brown (a lifelong worshipper at St Barnabas' Church until his death in 1937) used to walk from his home in the High Street to watch the new church taking shape in the late 1860s. But he and his brother were allowed to do so only if they promised their parents that they would 'keep to the middle of the road and pay no attention to anything they heard or saw on the way. Furthermore on no account were they to go at night, for they would probably have rats' tails and oyster shells thrown at them, so deep seated was the general distrust of Jericho.' By this time, the distinction between the canal and Jericho had become blurred. During the exceptional 'Town and Gown' disturbances of 1867, for instance, the *Daily Telegraph* claimed that 'Oxford has suburbs, like the one nicknamed "Jericho", containing plenty of rough bargees and railway labourers glad to "lick a lord", and the young and hot blood of the students regards it as an equal luxury to thrash a cad'.

Jericho's reputation may be one reason why the Canal Company consistently rebuffed all requests for easier access. In 1867 Richard Gillett advised the Mayor of Oxford of the Company's refusal to erect a footbridge over the canal at Jericho, because 'there are those whose interest in the bridge is considerable who entertain objections to its erection'. Among these objectors was the London and North Western Railway Company, many of whose employees almost certainly lived in Jericho, and for whom easier access would have been a real boon. Nonetheless, it must be remembered that both the canals and the railways were run by private companies, understandably reluctant to allow unrestricted public access to their properties.

Their reluctance was maintained. In 1924, for instance, we find the *Oxford Mail* reporting on unheeded demands for a bridge to allow Jericho's railwaymen an easier route to work, and to give its children access to the sports ground and bathing place at Tumbling Bay. Then in 1928, the Company rejected the application of the City Engineer to erect a bridge, because 'there is no public right of way on the towpath of the canal, and there is already a private ferry at this place for which a small charge is made by the tenant of the Company's house there'. The ferry in question had operated since 1868, seemingly introduced therefore as a concession to the Mayor's 1867 request for a bridge. It duly remained the only means of crossing for nearly a hundred years. By the time a bridge was finally built in 1972, times had moved on. Jericho no longer had a monopoly on housing railway workers, nor was Tumbling Bay a suitable place to learn to swim, and the canal was little more than a neglected and unwholesome ditch. Little wonder, therefore, that the long-awaited bridge acquired the tag of 'a bridge to nowhere'.

Herbert's Ferry

The first Jericho ferry was established by J. Bricknell, who paid the Company £15 p.a. from 1868 on. It operated from the site now occupied by College Cruisers, overlooked by a Canal Company property called Ferry House. According to Ted Harris, a Combe Road resident since the 1940s, the scullery now forms part of the single-storey brick building used as College's office. A handwritten note in a 1924 Company book of plans says that Ferry House was purchased on 15 January 1882 for £415, and that the first tenant, Richard Howkins, was installed in March 1883, when the rent for the ferry had gone down to £12 p.a.

The ferry itself was a large chain-operated punt. It was always known to Ted Harris and others as Herbert's Ferry, after the occupant of Ferry House from 1895 to 1927, a coalmerchant called William Herbert. He and his wife were recalled in Miss Hawtrey's *Scrapbook* by 'Mrs D.', who moved to Canal Street as a girl in 1897, and remembered that 'at the bottom of their garden was the house where tolls were paid. Barges went up and

The Jericho ferry and Ferry House, from *Isis and Thamesis* by Alfred J. Church (1886). The ferry was started in 1868, and continued for nearly 100 years, mostly under the popular name of 'Herbert's Ferry' in honour of the couple who ran it from 1895 until the 1920s.

down continually bringing cargoes of slate and coal, and the old mill donkey walked along in front – the whole effect being very picturesque. There was a ferry, looked after by a Mr & Mrs Herbert, who took you across for a halfpenny.'

When the *Scrapbook* was compiled in 1956, Mrs D. (Miss Hawtrey did not give the full names of any of her informants) had been living in Ferry Road, the name by which Combe Road was then known. Called Ferry Place for two or three years when it was first laid out, then Ferry Road from 1890, this short street was renamed in 1959 after Thomas Combe, who provided the funds for the construction of St Barnabas' Church. The new name was needed to avoid confusion with another Ferry Road in Marston. Ted Harris remembered the residents getting quite indignant about this, because the Marston ferry had long since vanished, while the Jericho one was still very much in evidence, and continued into the 1960s. The two houses closest to the canal are the focus of the Inspector Morse story *The Dead of Jericho*.

St Barnabas' Church

Thomas Combe (1796–1872) had joined the Oxford University Press in 1838, and went on to become its Superintendent. He also owned Wolvercote Paper Mill from 1855 onwards. He and his wife Martha (1806–1893) were great local benefactors, and to cater for the perceived spiritual needs of the growing population of Jericho, Combe commissioned the construction of St Barnabas' Church on the basis that no funds should be wasted on the external appearance. The church was built on land donated by the Ward family, seemingly Henry Ward's son, George (1823–1887), who was an ironmonger. Thomas Combe too had associations with metalworking: his father in Leicester had been a dealer in iron (as well as a bookseller), and his wife's father, John Edwards (c.1772–1857), had been in business with William Carter, who established the foundry in Jericho.

In announcing the laying of the church's foundation stone on 24 April 1868, *Jackson's Oxford Journal* commented, 'Not many years ago, the meadows in this direction, which were flooded in winter, were known as "Wards Fields", the ground was then taken for gardens, and within the last three or four years these

have given way to streets'. Canal Company correspondence at this time refers to 'rough rubble stone which is being brought from Enslow for the new church at Jericho' and to permission for the builder, Joseph Castle, 'to continue the road to the canalside' so that he could 'cart direct away from the boats'. The Company felt compelled to write to him in June 1868 to ask him to address 'the great injury to the canal from boys throwing large quantities of your gravel into it at the spot where you are building the new church at Jericho'. The church was consecrated in 1869. As a young man, the novelist Thomas Hardy had worked for Sir Arthur Blomfield, the architect of St Barnabas', which is clearly the inspiration for St Silas' Church in *Jude the Obscure* (1896). Hardy describes it as 'the church of ceremonies', an allusion to St Barnabas' importance within the Oxford Movement.

The church served to emphasise Jericho's notoriety, since it attracted widespread suspicion for its ritualistic, Anglo-Catholic tendencies. It also represented the closest connection yet between the canal and the Jericho community. The Ward family was linked with the canal, of course, and the first sacristan of this temple of High Anglican worship provided a further bond. John Foster retired from the post in 1909, at the age of 69, and the *Scrapbook* recounts that 'He built himself a little house opposite the church (47 Cardigan Street) and had the sign "Sacristan and Coal Merchant" on his front door. His coal was kept on the yard across the road and he vended it in the evenings.' The ferryman William Herbert also called himself a coalmerchant, and also had strong allegiances to the church. A plaque inside commemorates the deaths of two of Herbert's sons, William Percival (aged six) and Montague George (aged seven), in 1902 and 1905 respectively, and describes the Herbert boys as 'bearers of the incense boat'. The younger brother was almost certainly named after the greatly appreciated first vicar of St Barnabas', Montague Noel, who remained for some 30 years. One, perhaps both, of the Herbert boys reputedly drowned in the canal.

Opposite: St Barnabas' Church, drawn by J. Fisher 'in memory of the founder Thomas Combe Esq', c.1872. The boat's name is 'Beatrice', and on the cabin is written 'W. Ward, Oxford'.

Copyright: Bodleian Library, University of Oxford. G.A. Oxon a69 p.23

Corporation (Henry Ward's) Wharf

At the time of writing, the church overlooks a scene of desolation and neglect. This sad state of affairs ill-befits a location which has been both integral to Jericho's distinctive character for nearly

200 years and also of wider importance to Oxford as a whole. For it was the Jericho wharves which were considered 'ample alternative accommodation … for delivery and stacking of all goods carried on the Canal' when the Oxford Canal Company first contemplated its strategic withdrawal from the city centre in 1927. The site had been acquired by the Company in 1868, from Henry Ward's sons, George and Henry (1808–1874), and later became known as Nelson Street Wharf or Corporation Wharf.

A second Jericho ferry crossed the canal here during and after the Second World War. This was a punt provided by Oxford Corporation specifically to enable children from Jericho to go swimming at Tumbling Bay (see page 75). There was a particularly strong collective memory among his contemporaries of a pushy lad called Davis who, while elbowing his way to the front of the ferry, fell in with his war-time gas-mask on, and emerged sodden and breathless to earn the long-lived nickname of 'Diver Davis'.

In the previous century, Jericho's children were treated to rather longer boat trips. The *Scrapbook* notes the St Barnabas' school log-book entry for 18 July 1876, for instance: 'The boys assembled at eleven for church and after a short service marched to the boat headed by the school drum and fife band, and started for Nuneham about 12 o'clock.' But girls did go too! Mrs A., aged 85, who lived with her parents and six brothers and sisters in Walton Well Road when young, confirmed this yearly treat: 'The drum and fife band escorted them to Folly Bridge. At Sandford Lock a pause for a bun and ginger beer! While on the lawn at Nuneham there was a good tea.' Nuneham House, on the river between Oxford and Abingdon, was a favourite destination for all kinds of boat outings from Oxford (most famously those taken by Lewis Carroll with Alice Liddell and her sisters). Thomas Combe, who financed the building of the school (in Great Clarendon Street, on land once owned by the Wards) used to go on these annual excursions himself in its early years.

Currently, Henry Ward's old wharf, the Great Bear Meadow of old, retains three reminders of the canal's working heritage: a former forge (probably built to coincide with the Canal Company's inter-war move from the city centre), an older small building, possibly used as stables, and a modern inlet for docking. The ugly wooden fence has been in place since 2006, representing the first time since the canal's origins that boats have been unable to moor here, and the first time since at least the 1970s that they have been denied access for essential repairs. Ironically, the cause of this depressing situation is the very organisation which was supposed to protect the extraordinary heritage that our canal system represents: British Waterways, which decided to sell the entire site, including the greater part of that leased by College Cruisers, for development in 2005. How hollow the optimism expressed in the first edition of this book now sounds. Far from deserving congratulations in anticipation of 'including the community's wishes within the design brief for any potential developers', BW actually resisted repeated entreaties to retain part of the site for boat-repair purposes, and in 2006 employed heavy-handed methods, and profligate use of public funds, to evict boaters who had continued to work at the site in desperation at the lack of any alternative. A number of these boaters had 'Agenda 21' residential moorings, instigated by BW between Jericho and Duke's Cut in 2002, partly on the very basis of there being a nearby yard to service this low-impact housing! A unified resistance arose, comprising boaters, Jericho residents, and St Barnabas' Church, all of whom cherished the distinctive contribution that the boatyard made to Jericho, even if 'Brutish Waterways' did not! There had already been one costly and troublesome Public Inquiry in 2005; the resistance at a second one held in 2008 was still more effective.

At the forefront of the campaign was the Oxford author Philip Pullman, whose books *Northern Lights* and *Lyra's Oxford* incorporate an imaginary yet familiar Jericho, with its 'gyptian families, who lived in canal-boats, came and went with the spring and autumn fairs, and were always good for a fight', and where 'the wharves along the waterfront … were bright with gleaming harness and loud with the clop of hooves and clamour of bargaining'. Pullman's assessment (in December 2007) of the second planning proposal encapsulated many eloquent objections in observing that the scheme displayed *'an arrogance of scale, a contempt for one section of the community, namely the boat-owners, and an ignorance of the true nature and value of urban life'*.

The 'Battle of Jericho' has required immense sacrifices of time and money for countless individuals, and although the site remains a derelict and forlorn eyesore, this does nonetheless represent a victory of sorts. With the bankruptcy of the second developer, the opportunity remains for a community-purchase of the site. Undoubtedly, this will require gestures of philanthropy in keeping with those of the Combes and the Wards in the 19th century, but the will is there, and with it the sustained hope that the recent years will constitute only a temporary severing of two centuries of canal-related economic activity on the site.

Residential and hire boats in Jericho

Before leaving Jericho, it is pertinent to dwell on the aspect of canal-based commerce which saved the canals from extinction in the late 20th century, namely the leisure trade. Nationally, the origins of this can be traced to the publication of L.T.C. Rolt's 1944 book *Narrowboat*, which recorded a journey through 'uncharted home-waters less familiar than the Solomon Islands'. Rolt's achievements proved that the canals were still navigable *and* pleasurable, despite decades of neglect, and led eventually to the formation of the Inland Waterways Association (IWA), still the principal pressure group in the sector. Rolt also demonstrated that a boat could be a home. For both these aspects of boating over the last 50 years – residential and recreational – Jericho has proved a veritable haven.

A post-1945 housing shortage in Oxford encouraged many people to take to floating homes. The trend continued in proportion to improvements to the canal system as a whole, and by the mid-1980s a large number of residential boats had accumulated on the stretch of canal near Jericho. These boats were the cause of some concern to the authorities, and a well-publicised dispute over mooring rights ensued. In 1985 a councillor was quoted as saying, 'We do not want a boat city in Oxford, and are determined that this little flotilla is going to have to sail on.' The British Waterways Board was equally uncompromising, offering no better solution than to threaten the boat dwellers with eviction and confiscation of their vessels. It was a time when to boaters BW meant 'We Trouble You'!

Local residents tended to side with the boating community. In 1985 an IWA spokesperson had said of the canal: 'People tell us that they never walk along there because it's so nasty'. Yet by 1987 a letter from the Jericho Residents' Association printed in the *Oxford Times* was claiming that the presence of the boats 'positively increases the amenity value and security of the canal bank in our area. They have turned an often dangerous towpath into an area integrated with Jericho.' This sentiment shows a certain historical continuity. Relations between the working boatpeople and bankside residents seem generally to have been good – they were to some extent mutually dependent, after all – and the prejudices against boatpeople have tended to emanate from much farther afield.

In 1989 the 'saga of the Oxford boatpeople' was partly resolved with the establishment of authorised moorings at Hythe Bridge Arm, but not before it had gained national notoriety (and even international opprobrium, with a report by a Soviet film crew on the trail of an unacceptable face of capitalism!). Oxford has an unusually high proportion of residential boats. It could be said that these boat dwellers represent the perpetuation of the working boatpeople's traditional lifestyles, in terms of their boats being year-round homes. Meanwhile, a handful of working boats

Passengers replacing freight in an early example of the canal's transition to the tourism and leisure trade, pictured on Hythe Bridge Arm in 1957.

Copyright: Oxfordshire County Council, Oxfordshire History Centre

sustain the memory of the canals' original purpose, and locally 'Dusty', alias Mark Boardman, admirably operates a year-round service between Cropredy and Oxford, supplying boats with coal, gas, and diesel, whatever the weather. But the mainstay of modern canalboat commerce is holiday hire. This is popular today, but in 1957 the Oxford Canal Association noted the four hotel-boats and one hire-boat operator then on the southern Oxford Canal as a 'comparatively recent innovation'. This Association was formed as a result of a public meeting at Oxford Town Hall on 3 June 1955. It was chaired by John Betjeman (see page 21), who described the British Transport Commission, the body calling for the closure of the canal (in a phrase which most would say could equally be applied to the Commission's most recent successor), as 'this high-handed, incompetent and cruel thing'. Subsequently, as *The Oxford Times* reported on 2 March 1956, over 10,000 people signed the Association's petition to save the canal. The campaign must have seemed a forlorn task at times. Mr W.E. Pill was the resident keeper at Duke's Lock cottage in 1955, when the paddles on both gates at Louse (i.e. Isis) Lock were left open, and the entire canal below Wolvercote Lock was drained overnight. His comment, that 'Fortunately, there were no boats in the canal' at the time, tells its own tale.

Denis Wise, whose familiarity with the canal in Jericho encompassed more than four decades, recalled one horse-drawn boat which operated passenger trips from Hythe Bridge to Wolvercote and Thrupp around 1960. The owners had installed bus seats, charging 10s 6d return, including refreshments. The horse fell into Isis Lock on one occasion, according to Denis, and had to be rescued by the Fire Brigade! Jack and Rose Skinner's first butty, *Gertrude*, was put to the same use, according to Kingsley Belsten in *The Oxford Times* of 29 May 1964, meaning that *Gertrude* 'was the last horse-drawn boat seen at Oxford'. Jack's uncle, Joe, meanwhile, with his wife Rose, had the distinction of running the last mule-drawn freight boat, *Friendship*.

The canal's transition from a working environment to a largely leisure-based resource has been relatively sudden. The 1990s saw another major change, this time in the attitude of the Oxford public, spurred on by the equally unprecedented interest of property developers in canalside land. An event organised in April 1995 by Oxford Friends of the Earth, the boating community, and nearby residents' associations highlighted the likely cumulative impact of developments then proposed for nine separate sites along the canal corridor. Nearly a thousand people assembled in a human chain running the full one and a half miles' length of these combined proposals, and a petition signed by some 900 people asked for sensitive treatment of the sites and for traffic to be kept to a minimum. This unprecedented unity of 'boat and bank' showed clearly that appreciation of the environmental, recreational, and heritage value of the canal had spread wider than ever before – although sadly, not quite far enough to prevent the proliferation of new housing that now occupies a huge swathe of land between the railway and the canal. 'Brown-field' sites though these were, this intensive flood-plain development seems certain to have contributed to the flooding that Oxford has experienced in recent years – in 2007 and 2008 in particular – and will doubtless continue so to do.

The front page of the *Oxford Mail* of 3 April 1995 after an unprecedented, but ultimately impotent, show of public concern over intensive developments proposed for land alongside the canal.

Copyright: Oxford & County Newspapers/ Oxford Mail.

The walk from the 'bridge to nowhere' has taken us along a narrow strip of land with the canal on one side, and a stream on the other. This watercourse, bounded by a mixture of mature woodland and new back gardens, was the main course of the Thames up to the end of the 18th century, flowing from the southern extent of Port Meadow at Medley, to continue southwards through Oxford to join today's Thames above Folly Bridge. This course, past the ancient mill once attached to Oxford Castle, has earned it the name of Castle Mill Stream. For a few years in the early 1790s, the sight of a Thames barge and a canal narrowboat moving side by side down the two waterways towards Hythe Bridge must have been a common one. It is impossible to say whether a sense of competition or compatibility would have prevailed during such chance encounters, but the occasion would certainly have given opportunities for an exchange of ideas and news between people from very different parts of the country. Such fleeting contact, even through to the 20th century, was necessarily often the way that friendships were made and inter-family loyalties and romances established. The canal's arrival meant that names traditionally associated with the fishing and boating communities of Oxford would from now on mingle with those of the Midlands. At the same time, the wharves of Oxford would increasingly ring with accents from the West Country and South Wales, through the vector of the Thames & Severn Canal, which had connected with the upper Thames at Lechlade in 1789. It was a time of exciting change. But also, as will be seen in the case of the boating families of Upper Fisher Row, a time of some friction as well.

Isis Lock to Hythe Bridge Street

Isis (Louse) Lock

The picturesque Isis Lock, marking the junction of the Oxford Canal and River Thames, has suffered a sinister, unsavoury reputation which belies the tranquillity of its present-day setting. Today the lock is a narrow one; that is, seven feet wide, the breadth which distinguishes a narrowboat from a barge, but it was originally designed specifically to allow the broader river barges access to the canal's terminal wharves beyond Hythe Bridge. The Company's earliest mention of it comes in a resolution of 20 August 1793 to build a chamber lock 'at the most convenient place near the Oxford Wharf to communicate with the River Thames, and that Mr Daniel Harris of the castle be employed

Isis Lock Bridge dates from 1844, the same year that the lock was reduced in width. This view from 1998 hints at the earlier isolation of the locality, but since the picture was taken, Rewley Park estate has been built on the land in the background. The bridge to the left leads to the Sheepwash Channel over Castle Mill Stream. It was built in 1851, to enable towhorses to reach the main Thames.

Photo: Mark Davies

to build same'. Harris was a remarkable figure. In respect of the waterways, it was as an engineer, architect, and builder that he figured most prominently, but he had other skills too, and the reference to 'the castle' is explained by his role as governor of Oxford Castle Gaol from 1786 to 1809. In this capacity, he was able to supply cheap, convict labour to excavate and construct the lock. More about Harris appears on page 76.

The original means by which boats moved between the canal and the Thames had been an unsatisfactory, single-gated lock immediately to the north of Hythe Bridge. The location of Isis Lock was decided only after the connecting Thames stream of the Sheepwash Channel had been confirmed as a feasible means of navigation (see page 73). Harris' prisoners began work on the new lock – referred to in the Canal Company's ledgers simply as 'Oxford Lock' – in 1795. It became fully operational in 1797. At about the same time, between 1793 and 1802, the Company purchased a number of river barges, specifically for onward conveyance on the Thames of goods destined as far as London. As a trading destination, Oxford must have been less than ideal. The demand for coal was probably consistently high on the basis of innumerable college fireplaces alone, but return loads were very scarce. Once the Company acquired a stake in the onward river trade, with wharves at Abingdon, Wallingford, and Reading, a broad-entry lock became all the more essential.

The lock chamber was narrowed, and slightly realigned, as part of a major programme of improvements undertaken by the Company in Oxford between 1842 and 1844. The timing is significant. 1844 was the year when Oxford's first railway station opened, near Folly Bridge. After having it broadly all their own way for 50 years, the proprietors of the canal had obviously foreseen the end of the connecting river trade and a consequent need to rationalise their own concerns. The narrowing of the lock was therefore presumably done with two economies in mind: to reduce water wastage and remove the need to monitor barge traffic coming off the Thames. The importance of the Oxford Canal as part of the shortest water route from the Midlands to London had in any case been shortlived. As early as 1805 the wider, more direct, Grand Union Canal from London to

A British
Waterways
Board work gang
replacing the lock
gates at Isis Lock
in the 1960s. A
water tank and
railway sidings
can be seen in the
background.

Photo: Fred Hann

Birmingham deprived it of this status, and with the increasing competition of road and rail, a significant fall in river trade was almost inevitable. The decision to use less water seems symbolic: an attempt to stem the outflow of lifeblood from a transport system which would soon fail to match its competition. Or a case of 'closing the lock gate after the towhorse has bolted' perhaps!

Whatever, it is to the lasting benefit of later generations that the Company was still prepared to add style to its utilitarian structures. The same year that Isis Lock was narrowed, in 1844, its original wooden bridge was replaced by the striking wrought-iron construction (Number 243) that we see today. The Company had no real need to lavish funds on such a fine structure, yet the pride it took in its trade is exemplified by the bridge, which stands as an evocative testimony to the success of the massive undertaking begun by the Canal Company back in 1769. In contrast, the canal bridges of more recent times seem to testify only to an emphasis on cost-cutting over long-term heritage.

Frederick Wood was the engineer responsible for the 1844 changes to Isis Lock, and the result inspired the novelist William Black to describe it in 1888 as 'a little toy-box kind of a basin'. This phrase – from *The Strange Adventures of a Houseboat*, Black's fact-based story of an epic 300-mile round trip – is still apt more than a century later.

The reality of the lock's past is less whimsical, however, as it has been the scene of numerous drownings. Those we know about occurred only once the lock had been narrowed. In 1866, for instance, a travelling salesman from Northampton was drowned after falling into the lock. Hearing cries of distress, the boatman James Beesley and his father (of Upper Fisher Row) steered their punt to the lock, but arrived too late. It was also Beesley (1841–1900) who discovered the body of a Christ Church undergraduate called Brookes in the lock in December 1868, his suspicions having been aroused when he saw a hat floating on the water. In both cases, *Jackson's* reported, 'the victims were supposed to have been precipitated from the towing path into the water by stumbling in the dark against a wooden T-cross placed midway on the lock side by the Canal Company'. Soon after, the Local Board suggested that this bollard 'seemed to be left there as a sort of man trap', and recommended its removal.

Ray Titcomb, growing up in Upper Fisher Row in the late 1940s, recalled the frequency with which drowned corpses were carried along the towpath, and Colin Tustin, his brother-in-law, said it was much the same when his family moved back to the Row in 1953, remembering that *'in the first 10 or 12 years after we moved here there was at least one drowning a year'.* Ted Harris also remembered *'ever such a lot of people drowning'.* In a place spurned by the general population, it is not surprising to learn that there have been cases of assault too. Ted Harris remembered that a Canal Street resident, Alderman Smewin, was nearly fatally beaten by American servicemen during the war, and that all the trees were cut down in the 1950s after a spate of attacks on women.

In accounts of all of the mid-19th-century instances of drowning, most accidental, but some evidently suicides, the lock was consistently referred to as 'Louse Lock'. The earliest printed use of this name appears in *Jackson's* of 18 April 1840, in relation to an unproven charge of stealing coal against Abel Beesley of Fisher Row. Older residents and the boating fraternity have always known it as Louse Lock. Della James, born and raised in Upper Fisher Row, said she *'had never known it was called anything else'*; the Oxford Canal Association referred to the Castle Mill Stream by Isis Lock as 'Louse stream' in 1957; and the *Shell Book of Inland Waterways* proffers Louse as the name as late as 1975, adding that it was 'more politely' known as Isis. The lock's less polite name might conceivably have derived from its early association with prisoners as well as with boatmen (the former probably as louse-ridden as any of that period, and the latter mistakenly assumed to be so). However, the name seems likely to have a more prosaic origin. One of the Canal Company's handwritten 1840 Chain Survey books dubs the lock 'Lowkes Lock'. Locks and bridges were often named after local landowners, benefactors, or notable employees. The Lowkes in question seems likely to have been the J. Lowkes who moved various cargoes for the Company from at least 1830 to 1843, and who regularly delivered coal direct to the Company's offices in Oxford. From this fact, one might conclude that Lowkes was a 'Number One', a self-employed boat-owner, enjoying a certain elevated trust from the Company, but the stronger likelihood is that he was the land-based owner of the boats making the deliveries. Possibly he was connected with the mercer, John Lowkes, who was the business partner of one of the three original Canal Company treasurers appointed in 1769. Whoever he was, we shall never know if he would have felt proud that the place still carries echoes of his name, or upset at the unfortunate corruption of it! Whatever, nowadays the lock is no longer the 'dismal' place to which Ray Titcomb's mother forbade him to go – ineffectively, in fact, since leaping the lock was considered a rite of passage to gang membership in his schooldays. And not everyone was deterred. Nancy Sherratt and her sisters thought of it always as a 'lovely' place. Having a wharfinger for a father (see page 57) made them perceive the canal differently, seeing it, and its associated structures and characters, as comforting rather than alien. And not every mishap there ended in tragedy. There have been numerous cases of life-saving heroism too. Often it was boatmen or fishermen who were involved, but it was a passer-by, a Mr Cutliffe, who was the earliest identified, administering successful mouth-to-mouth resuscitation on a five-year-old child called Austin, who had been 'brought to the bank, apparently dead' near Louse Lock in July 1852.

In contrast to its 'lousy' past, Isis Lock now welcomes thousands of visitors a year. Much as the presence of residential boats in Jericho had done in the 1980s, the establishment of permanent moorings along Hythe Bridge Arm in 1989 gave pedestrians a new confidence. Today, new housing has sprung up to the west of Castle Mill Stream, where semi-mature woodland had established itself by the mid-1990s. Today's circumstances exhibit a certain irony. For generations the reputation of the working boatpeople seems certain to have played its part in keeping the public away, yet now the presence of boats – residential this time – provides reassurance and interest. Meanwhile, the new housing has been built on old railway sidings. Despite everything, Isis Lock has defied both the railway and the doubters who might once have closed it for good, leaving it still a pivotal gateway to an inland waterway system stretching for more than 2,000 miles.

The canal towpath continues straight on over Wood's 1844 iron bridge along Hythe Bridge Arm to the city. The orientation of the bridge, skewed originally for the benefit of horses, has resulted in unforeseen happy consequences for today's users of cycles, prams, and wheelchairs. The footbridge over the Castle Mill Stream to the right was built by the Great Western Railway Company in 1851 'exclusively for the use of boathorses passing from the Canal to the River towpath'. Prior to this, it would seem that the horses were obliged to take a long detour along the canal to Hythe Bridge Street, then along the Botley Road, and back along the river towpath, to rejoin their boats at the far end of the Sheepwash Channel.

Hythe Bridge Arm

To continue along the Thames route from Isis Lock, via the Sheepwash Channel, turn to page 73.

The canal which had been started near Coventry in 1769 had got as far as Banbury by 1778. With mounting costs and little income, further progress was slow, and it took until 1789 before the canal reached the boundaries of urban Oxford. To complete the final section, a strip of land was purchased from Worcester College to take the cut via what is now known as Hythe Bridge Arm to a terminus beyond Hythe Bridge Street.

The purchase from Worcester College was completed on 16 July 1788. As a concession, the Canal Company agreed to provide the 'Provost, Fellows and Scholars with a passage for a boat into the said Canal and from thence into the Thames and Isis from time to time and at all times hereafter without paying any thing for the same'. This stipulation was rescinded in 1796. Many years later, when the Company was selling off its central holdings in 1937, the College paid £500 to buy back 'two roods and 28 perches' (a rood being equal to 40 perches, or a quarter of an acre) of its former land along the eastern edge of the canal.

Later the canal was blocked off at Hythe Bridge, as a result of the sale of the New Road and Hythe Bridge Basins to William Morris, Lord Nuffield. Unsurprisingly this near-stagnant dead-end had little to commend it, and by the early 1970s it was summed up by a local newspaper as a 'stinking ditch full of weeds, rubbish and empty bottles thrown in by local layabout alcoholics'. The canal as a whole rated little better at this time, and phrases such as 'Oxford's slum canal', 'a civic disgrace', and 'total squalor' were typical. John Liley, one of that small band of determined enthusiasts to whom we owe so much for proving that the decaying system still had a future, captured the general opinion: 'dead dog country', he called it in 1971, 'spurned by the Oxonians'. Indeed, such had been the case for some time. The book *Idle Women* tells the story of an all-women boatcrew recruited by the Ministry of Labour during the last war. In it, Susan Woolfit records that having moored up 'somewhere behind Worcester College' on their first trip to Oxford, she and her crew lost their way in the city, and found little assistance from local inhabitants, who 'seemed to be entirely ignorant of the presence of a canal in the city'. Jack and Rose Skinner were generous in their praise of these all-women crews, 'trainees' as they were known. Jack thought they were *better than all the men put together*', partly because they were more willing to listen to advice – although they fell in the Skinners' esteem because of their refusal to dress up on the rare occasions when they found time to socialise together. The boatpeople were always careful to look smart at public events, and were embarrassed by the scruffy working clothes that the middle-class trainees chose to wear.

The contrast between the bare basics of the narrowboats and the grand Worcester College buildings makes it easy to imagine a history of friction between the erudite scholars and the illiterate working boatpeople. Jack's recollections suggest otherwise, however – by the middle of the 20th century, at least. The canals had played their part in the war, and there was perhaps a general softening of opinion about those who had kept them running. According to Jack's experience, there was a mutual respect between these two very different sections of society, and he also perceived nothing but acceptance from the city's shopkeepers, even if he was sometimes '*black as a crow*' from coaldust!

At another level, however, canal and college were very much at odds. For more than a century the Canal Company and the College argued about the detrimental effect of the canal on the drainage of Worcester's fields. The canal was constructed with a wooden culvert to take water from the College under both the canal and Castle Mill Stream to empty into Beesley's Lasher, on the Wareham Stream. This worked well for about 50 years, but from the 1840s Worcester's meadows started to flood with ever greater frequency. This led the College to import tens of thousands of tons of soil to raise the level of their fields. It took until 1913 for the Company's obligation to be established in law, and for truly effective measures to be taken – so effective indeed that they

'Worcester College (from High Bridge)' by J. & H.S. Storer c.1813. The tall mast of the vessel on the canal reveals it as a barge from the river. The weir to the left marks the approximate location of the original connecting lock.

Copyright: Bodleian Library, University of Oxford. G.A. Oxon a.61.19

seem likely to have caused the demise of Plato's Well. This ancient water source, lying within Worcester's grounds near Hythe Bridge Street, was the lowest in a sequence of springs – including those at Aristotle Lane and Walton Well – emanating from the gravel terrace which lies parallel to the canal. The well had been described by Herbert Hurst as 'beautiful' and 'bountiful' as late as 1899, but subsequently is heard of no more.

At the time of writing, the line of residential boats along Hythe Bridge Arm includes several with claims to a working past: *Kilsby* began life as a Fellows, Morton & Clayton freight carrier in 1912; *Heron* was built (as *Caleb*) for the London, Midland, and Scottish Railway Co. in 1929, and acquired its current name in 1955 when it was bought by the Willow Wren Carrying Company; and *Ben* (a modern name) was a Birmingham Canal Navigation boat, with an inner hull dating back to 1873, making it one of the oldest on the whole canal system.

'The Armchair Weir'

The early 19th-century brick weir at the canal end is known as the 'Armchair Weir', on account of its shape when viewed from Upper Fisher Row. It marks the spot where a stream from

Worcester College formerly found its way to the river. From early maps it would seem that the run-off from Plato's Well once contributed to this stream, and that this was the intended access point for the college boat mentioned in the original 1788 agreement, as this was the site of the lock which preceded Isis Lock as the junction with the Thames. This simple lock is clearly seen in a painting of about 1790 by Michael Angelo Rucker (in the possession of the Museum of Oxford), showing a brick structure crossed by a wooden footbridge, and with a single pair of movable gates, set at an angle to the canal. Subsequent views indicate its continued presence in an increasingly dilapidated state for another 40 years or so. It was in any case never satisfactory. Robert Whitworth surveyed the whole canal in January 1791, and advised improvements to 'the Gates that let the boats down from the Canal into the River, as I observe it is very tedious to pass a boat from one to the other'. Tedious *and* disruptive! A prime reason for building the double-gated pound lock which became Isis Lock, according to the Company minutes of 28 September 1792, was the 'injuries which have been repeatedly experienced from letting water out of the Basin'. The simple lock depicted in Rooker's painting would have done exactly that – allowing boats to leave or enter the canal, not without difficulty, on a surge of water, much as the early Thames flash locks had.

The Boatmen's Floating Chapel

For three decades of the 19th century something remarkable could be seen upstream of the weir on the Castle Mill Stream. It was a box-shaped, wooden structure known as the Boatmen's Floating Chapel, and as so often in matters relating to the canal in 19th-century Oxford, the Ward family was at the heart of it. Henry Ward (c.1781–1852) provided the hull of an old Thames barge and paid for the construction work, while his son William (1807–1889) assumed the role of treasurer. The Chapel was tangible evidence of the family's concern for the moral and spiritual wellbeing of the men and women who worked for them, and shows a mellowing of attitude since 1794, when Henry's father, William Ward (1744–1815), put his corporate name to a notice in *Jackson's* offering a reward for information relating to the frequent theft of 'coals, grain, goods and merchandise from out of our boats, by the persons employed to hawl them'. William, who had been born in Staffordshire, was among the first merchants to occupy the canal's city terminus. The notice concluded sternly: 'In future we will not suffer our boat hawlers to bring any coals for their own use, as from experience we find that indulgence has been attended with great inconvenience, they having made that a pretext for selling coals on their voyage.' In his will, William described Henry with surprising candour as his 'natural born and adopted' son, while the 1851 census shows that he was born in the small Warwickshire canalside village of Hillmorton. In combination, these details, with the hint of 'wild oats' sown in passing, seem to imply that William may himself have once been a boatman.

When the Chapel was moved into position in June 1839, *Jackson's* praised Henry Ward with the words: 'It is gratifying in the extreme to see an individual devoting his time, his energies, and his means, towards the amelioration of that class of society whose inattention to religious duties he has had such ample opportunities of witnessing.' To address exactly this 'inattention', the Wards were prominent in calling for a national prohibition on the movement of boats on Sundays, and were among the very first employers to stop their own boatmen from doing so. This was of course highly relevant. The crews of narrowboats waiting to be offloaded at Oxford's central wharves on the Monday would have no excuse not to visit a Chapel moored only a few feet from the towpath on the preceding day!

The Chapel was consecrated on 29 December 1839 by the Bishop of Oxford. Its design was as important as its location. In *Recollections of Oxford*, G. V. Cox commended Henry Ward, 'the excellent father of an excellent family' for his perception in realising that 'the bargemen never did and never would present themselves *at a church* in their rough costume' but felt quite at home in a barge. The Chapel, 'in the Egyptian style', was 70 feet long by 14 feet wide. *Jackson's* commented on the vessel's 'chaste and elegant design … judiciously decorated with appropriate ornaments'. The builder was John Plowman, who had been Daniel Harris' business partner from 1812 to 1837 (once the latter had resigned from the

'The Shipman's Chapel' by Carl Rundt from *A Walk Round Oxford* (c.1850). Note the canal arch (far left), the old Hythe Bridge (replaced in 1861), St George's Tower (next to the unseen Castle Mill), and the boats for hire along Upper Fisher Row (also known as 'Pleasure-Boat Row'). It is likely that a Beesley or a Bossom would be among the residents gathered on the banks!

Castle Gaol), and his foreman prior to that. In the early years, according to the Chapel's published accounts, between 50 and 70 children attended the school, rising to over 100 in the 1850s, by which time it was operating daily, and admitting in addition local children who were not from the boats.

The Chapel was sufficiently permanent to be named on Hoggar's 1850 map, but despite contributions towards its upkeep from a range of subscribers (including the Wards, the Canal Company, and Christ Church, the college with responsibility for St Thomas' parish, in which the Chapel lay) the costs eventually became too burdensome, and the last services were held early in 1868. In a *Short Memoir* of Thomas Chamberlain, who served as vicar of St Thomas' parish for 50 years until his death in 1892 and was responsible for the Chapel in all but its first few years, its demise was summed up as: 'Being possessed of less endurance than the Vicar, and probably weary and disgusted with its poor surroundings, it quietly sank one Sunday morning. It was not worth raising.' The photographer Henry Taunt took a more positive line, saying that the Chapel had 'fulfilled her mission'. In fact, this was not strictly true, because a replacement was considered necessary. This time it was on dry land, built on the north side of Hythe Bridge Street, and doubled as a day school for infants and a night school for men. It was used for services until about 1892, and now provides services of a more tangible kind as a Thai restaurant.

Before stepping on to Hythe Bridge Street, it is worth pausing at the monument designed by William Bird. It commemorates the canal's 200th anniversary – well, almost! The Oxford Canal was finished by December 1789, but – possibly in keeping with the slow pace of life on the canals – this bicentennial monument was inaugurated in September 1993. Ray Titcomb remembered the days when the canal was completely blocked off here in about 1950. With the Basins drained of water, he and his schoolfriends carried floundering fish and eels from the mud on one side of Hythe Bridge to the canal on the other. The grassed area is the result of a job-creation scheme in the late 1970s, and it is thanks to the efforts of volunteers from the Inland Waterways Association that the Arm remains in use today, as it might well have been filled in at the same time. Its continued existence sustains the attractive notion that the Georgian basin might one day be reinstated as the canal's rightful terminus.

 ## The City

Hythe Bridge and New Road Wharves (The Basin)

On the southern side of Hythe Bridge Street is a car-park, the site of the canal's initial 1790 terminus. Before then, the land here seems to have comprised an uncultivated open space, a kind of no-man's land between two rather different Oxfords: the densely populated, unruly suburb of the parish of St Thomas and adjacent Castle Gaol, and the contrasting opulence of New Inn Hall Street and Worcester College. Part of this plot was described in Canal Company ledgers as 'Bossom's Garden'. The Bossoms were a prominent local family, whose influence on Oxford's waterway fortunes has been considerable. More about them, and their chief rivals for most of the 19th century, the Beesley family, appears in the section on Upper Fisher Row.

Daniel Harris' prisoners were called in to complete the construction of the canal and some of its terminal buildings – a dream job for Harris, presumably, in view of its proximity to the Gaol. Convict labour alone was obviously not enough, however, since the Company placed an advert in *Jackson's* of 14 June 1788 for 'cutters and labourers' to complete the canal. At the same time it advertised for boatbuilders, to build up to ten boats 70 feet long and seven feet wide.

The canal was finished in December 1789, and the first boat arrived on New Year's Day 1790. It was an understandable cause of excitement. *Jackson's* of 2 January 1790 reported:

> The Oxford Canal was yesterday opened by the arrival of upwards of two hundred tons of coals, besides corn and other effects.
> The first boat entered the bason [sic] a few minutes before twelve o'clock, displaying the union flag, and having on board the band of the Oxfordshire Militia. They were received by a vast concourse of people, with loud huzzas, and an ox having been roasted whole upon the wharf, on approaching, the band struck up The Roast Beef of England, a favourite tune, and well applied.

To continue past the canal's old terminus and on to the Canal Company's former headquarters, cross Hythe Bridge Street near the junction with Worcester Street. To continue towards the Thames path along Upper Fisher Row, turn to page 64.

A few days later, on 7 January 1790, the ledgers of the parish church of St Thomas show a payment of 5s for bellringing as part of the 'rejoicing at ye coals coming to Oxford to ye New Cannal Wharf'.

The canal's impact was immediate and immense. Coal was almost proverbially scarce in Oxford, so the prospect of plentiful, affordable supplies of it was a hugely significant event. For many of the poor, this significance was probably life-saving, for tradesmen it brought all kinds of new opportunities, and for the city as a whole it provided an economic fillip which saw property prices rise rapidly after a period of stagnation. For the affluent colleges, the canal's effect was probably minimal, save for those many academics in possession of soon-to-be precious share holdings.

In its early years, the Canal Company prospered. The huge construction costs meant that no dividends were paid out in the first few years, but receipts leapt from £5,500 in 1789 to £26,000 in 1796. Trade was such that a second wharf was needed, and the canal was extended under Worcester Street to new wharves lying where Nuffield College now stands. The labour again came from the conveniently located Castle Gaol, although not exclusively, since Daniel Harris advertised in 1793 for 'several rough carpenters, labourers and navigators', adding that 'Useful working men will find constant employ and good wages.' The double terminus was taken to its maximum extent early in 1801, with purchases of land with evocative (but now vanished) names such as 'Jews' Mount', 'Badcock's Garden', and 'The Folly'. The two wharves differentiated between merchandise at Hythe Bridge (where Pickford's had a major stake) and coal at New Road. A year earlier, with trade expanding, the Company had resolved to widen the arch of the bridge between their two terminal wharves 'so as to admit Thames barges into the new wharf', seeming to justify the decision to make Isis Lock wide enough to allow barge access. This little humpback bridge on Worcester Street survived until the construction of Nuffield College began on the New Road site around 1950.

Nancy Sherratt and her four sisters lived in a house immediately next to this bridge from 1922 until the wharves were sold in 1937. Although their house, 'Wharf House', was situated within the

Hythe Bridge site, her father, Bernard Robinson, was wharfinger at New Road, and she remembered how he would do the rounds of the dosshouses of St Thomas' parish whenever boats arrived, to enlist labour to unload them. Even in those depressed times, this hard, dirty, exposed work found few enthusiasts.

The Hythe Bridge site was run by Hubert Hawkins, and Nancy remembered her sisters' girlish infatuation with the handsome young man who used to load Hawkins' coalcart. It was pulled by an immensely patient, obedient horse called Blossom, which went all over Oxford to make deliveries. With the boaters themselves, the girls had little contact – although Nancy's father did regularly invite one man in for tea. They knew him only as 'Old Blower', on account of a slight speech defect and strong regional accent which, in combination with a liberal use of swear words, often had the girls in fits of discreetly shared mirth.

Despite the competition and lack of investment, the total tonnage carried on the Oxford Canal grew modestly until the Second World War, and the Company was still able to pay dividends to its shareholders even then. One reason was that a journey by boat was relatively smooth, making the canal a preferred choice for fragile cargoes (such as nitro-glycerine!). In addition, the canal basin offered superior storage facilities, notably a large pottery warehouse and Pickford's furniture depository, which straddled one line of the 'L', as Nancy Sherratt called it, the point where the canal branched within the Hythe Bridge site to enable boats to turn. Pickford's had been one of the largest canal carrying companies in the 19th century, and it was a murder on one of their passenger services in 1839 that inspired the Inspector Morse novel, *The Wench is Dead*, set fictionally on the Oxford Canal.

The Nuffield College buildings were completed in 1960, and through the gateway on Worcester Street a symbolic reminder of the site's former use can be seen in the form of the oblong pond within the college quad. Only two other clues remain. Next to The Duke's Cut pub (once The Queen's Arms) is a single blue-brick pillar, marking the wharf access gate from Park End Street. On the opposite side of the car-park, the bricks marking part of the canal's entrance arch under Hythe Bridge Street can be discerned in the wall.

At the time of writing, there is talk of opening up this bridge again, and reinstating the canal basin as a means of attracting more visiting boats to the city. It is a chance for Oxford to show its gratitude to this 200-year-old survivor, to acknowledge the part it played in the city's social and economic development, and to demonstrate that in the 21st century the canal is at last a resource to be respected, not neglected. The land is still owned by Nuffield College, the legacy of William Morris, whose eponymous motorcar provided the fortune which enabled its construction. Morris' intention had been to 'bridge the gap between industry and intellect', a sentiment which has echoes of the canal's original impact on Oxford. At a time when the mixed blessings of the motorcar are ever more apparent, it is probably not too fanciful to imagine that Morris would have approved of the revived fortunes of the workmanlike canal, were he alive today, and might even have welcomed the prospect of canalboats replacing the cars which occupy their more rightful territory.

Opposite:
New Road Wharf, 1930s. Canal House stands top right, slightly obscured by vegetation, and the new buildings of St Peter's College stand beyond Bulwarks Lane. Top left is the spire of the Wesley Memorial Church in New Inn Hall Street. The two boats are *Friendship* and *Elizabeth*, owned by Jack Skinner's uncle and aunt, Joe and Rose Skinner.

Copyright: British Waterways Archives

Canal House

Behind Nuffield College is the Canal Company's former head-quarters, Canal House. It is reached by crossing Worcester Street into George Street Mews, which runs alongside the College's northern wall. The Mews bends right to become Bulwarks Lane, an ancient, curving passage which follows the outer extent of the protective ditch which encircled the Castle Mound in mediaeval times. Canal House was designed in 1827 by Richard Tawney (1774–1832), who had been the Company's agent and engineer since 1794, and was a member of the family of entrepreneurs and philanthropists (with a background in the river trade) who were influential in the affairs of west Oxford for many generations. When Canal House was completed in 1829, the Company was approaching the peak of its success, and the proprietors evidently wanted to rival the pomp of Oxford's colleges with an ostentatious building of their own. Many shareholders had strong college connections anyway, of course, and perhaps felt a certain obligation to enhance the public profile of the mercantile world which the University was generally so reluctant to embrace.

To find Canal House, cross Worcester Street at the traffic lights and turn into the cobbled lane of George Street Mews.

The Oxford Canal Company cartouche on Canal House: the figure of Britannia and the city arms impaled with the arms of the University alongside the Church of St Mary the Virgin, the Radcliffe Camera, and a river barge with mast – an unlikely juxtaposition of church, trade, city, and academia, advertising a commercial joint venture.

Photo: Mark Davies

Above the Doric columns of the portico is evidence of a company brimming with confidence: a cartouche of Britannia and a river barge, together with the Radcliffe Camera and University Church of St Mary the Virgin. The cartouche is made of Coade stone, and had originally graced the Canal Company's first headquarters building, built by the prison governor Daniel Harris (see page 62). Harris – an artist as well as an artisan – may even have designed the cartouche (or seal, as it was called): when the Canal Company paid the Lambeth-based Coade Company £43 12s, the accompanying letter of 18 December 1797 shows that it was in settlement of the bill which had been 'sent to Mr Harris for the model of the company's seal'. Britannia's shield bears the arms of the city, impaled with the arms of the University, and is, quite literally, a sign of the times: a unique public proclamation of town and gown collaboration, inspired by a mutual dependence on coal.

Coal had been the unifying factor in an uneasy Oxford alliance some years earlier too. In November 1769, the very same month that construction of the canal began near Coventry, four representatives of the city (including Edward Tawney, the great uncle of Richard) and three from the University agreed to purchase barges to ship coal from London. Both parties, town and gown, had a vested interest in 'reducing the present exorbitant price of coals', yet only three years later, what would appear to be the same barge company was advertising the sale of its stock, under the supervision of Edward Tawney's brother, Richard. This sale was presumably in anticipation of the approaching canal. However, it was apparently not until a few years more, in December 1778, that *Jackson's* carried the first advertisement for 'Oxford Navigation Coals'. The supplier was Richard Ward, probably a relative of the canal-based Wards already referred to, and likely to be the same Richard Ward who ran road carriage services from St Giles at this time. The advertisement did appear only once though, suggesting that the practicalities of transferring coal from boats to wagons might actually have defeated his entrepreneurial ambition. By 1782, however, the Canal Company itself was advertising the availability of pit coal from its office in St Giles, and retained a 'Navigation Office' in the street until at least 1792.

Canal House is a curiously eccentric building. Its orientation makes it seem strangely reluctant to face the wharves that it was built to oversee, and while from Bulwarks Lane it makes no pretensions to be anything more than a two-storey, plain brick warehouse, from the opposite side it appears as a three-storey Georgian mansion, yet as a stone-built Greek temple from the front!

By the early 20th century, the building seems to have constituted little more than a maudlin reminder of former glories. An incident in E. Temple Thurston's 1911 book *The Flower of Gloster* is indicative. This was a time when the canal system was barely surviving, as illustrated by a conversation between Thurston and a lone Company employee based at Canal House. When asked what time of the year was the busiest, the clerk gestured to the flourishing garden outside and answered, 'the Spring'! The building was purchased by St Peter's College in 1961, and is now home to the College's Master.

For a longer view of Canal House, turn right at the end of Bulwarks Lane and proceed down New Road. Continue down New Road, if so desired, to join the river path back at Hythe Bridge Street (see page 64).

Wyaston (Linton) House

To reach Wyaston House, turn left at the end of Bulwarks Lane, walk through Bonn Square and turn left again into New Inn Hall Street. Wyaston House is set back from the road on the left, about half-way along.

Before the construction of Canal House, the Canal Company's headquarters had been a large, plain-fronted building in New Inn Hall Street. This had been erected on land formerly owned by William Jackson (1721–1795), the founder of *Jackson's Oxford Journal*. When Jackson died in 1795, the plot was one of a number of his possessions (including ten £100 Canal Company shares) advertised for auction in the edition of 11 July. The irrepressible Daniel Harris was asked to handle the purchase, the Company then ordering 'that a house and offices … with a room for the meetings of the committee according to the plan given by Mr Daniel Harris be built under the direction of the said Mr Harris'. This he had evidently done by 13 April 1796, when the first meeting was held in the building, though work continued well into 1797. Once the Company had transferred to Canal House, the censuses of 1841 and 1851 show that the old building became the private home of the third of the Company's identically named *de facto* Chairmen, David Durell (1798–1865). The Canal Company sold the house in 1878, when it became St Peter's Rectory, known soon after as Wyaston House, a name evidently derived from the new occupants, the Shirley family, who had ancestral connections with the village of Wyaston in Derbyshire. It was later renamed Linton House after Henry Linton, rector of the St Peter's parish for 21 years, and is now the entrance lodge to St Peter's College.

'We had fun sometimes too!'

Here, near the heart of the city, the canal trail ends. Having touched on some of the more significant and memorable moments in the 200-year history of this resilient waterway, it is time to find the river path and investigate the much older, more famous, and more cherished influence of the Thames on Oxford. First, though, because Jack and Rose Skinner rarely found reason to leave the cut for the Thames, it seems only right to leave the last word on the canal to two people for whom it really was their whole world.

In terms of boathandling pedigree, the respective families of both Jack and Rose (née Hone) Skinner are among the most remarkable. They and their kind were the ones who laboured in all weathers, who lived and loved, and were born and died on the cut; for whom it was a birthplace, a nursery, a classroom, a workplace, a morgue, and very occasionally a playground. Even after they had retired 'to the bank', Jack and Rose still went cruising whenever possible, although they couldn't get used to the idea that they could moor up whenever they wanted, and take things slowly! *'We can't stop! We've got to keep moving! In the old days, even on Sundays, we always kept moving,'* said Rose. But there were some moments of leisure too: 'sing songs' in the pubs with other boaters were fondly remembered, and the cinema or the theatre in Oxford (where they sometimes went to see the same show several times over). Rose also remembered vividly her girlhood wonderment at seeing her first elephant, tethered in the stables of the Basin when a circus was in town.

Despite the near-constant hard work, the hazards, the dirt, and the discomfort, they both said that given their time over again they would still have chosen to work the boats. With the waterways almost exclusively associated with leisure activities nowadays, it is pleasing to think that the likes of Jack and Rose, people without whom there might *be* no canal system for us to enjoy today, could sit back in their final years, smile, and remember *'We had fun sometimes too!'*

Jack and Rose Skinner on board Mark Davies' narrowboat in Oxford, June 1998.

Photo: Mark Davies

 Castle Mill Stream to Sheepwash Channel

Lower and Middle Fisher Rows

Back at Hythe Bridge, one of Oxford's most ancient points of entry, we begin to move from the narrow confines of the canal to the more pastoral waters of the Thames. The current bridge replaced a much earlier stone-built one in 1861, and over time the crossing point has been called both 'Hythe Bridge' and 'High Bridge' pretty much at random. The former is the intended name, since Oxford's original up-river wharf was here, its antiquity clear from the Saxon meaning of the word *hithe*, as a wharf or landing place. Oxford's other major river wharf, at Folly Bridge, handled goods coming from London. It would appear that small boats at least could once navigate between the two, using the lock (shown on the Christ Church map on page iv) where a sluice remains to this day, thereby avoiding the Castle Mill by using the Wareham Stream (another name of Saxon derivation). At least, that is the impression given by William Combe in his 1794 account, *An History of the River Thames*: immediately after Hythe Bridge 'the stream then bore us on to scenes which the most playful imagination could not hope to find in a navigable river, winding round a large and populous city. Banks thick with reeds, islets covered with osiers, and meadows fringed with willows, were the simple native objects which met the eye on every turn of the meandering stream.' By the time the German Carl Rundt chanced to enter Oxford via St Thomas' parish in about 1850, change was apparent. He described the suburb as 'the seat of industry and trade' – though at the same time, the many streams did inspire the artist in him to perceive similarities with Venice.

Downstream of Hythe Bridge are Middle and Lower Fisher Rows, and beyond that the site of the Castle Mill. A mill had operated here since Saxon times, and was finally demolished only in 1930. In 1954, the decaying 17th-century cottages which occupied much of Middle and Lower Fisher Rows were demolished, leaving only four houses at one end and The Nag's

Head pub at the other. Numbers 2 and 3 Lower Fisher Row were once almshouses, built by Edward Tawney (1735–1800) in 1797, and endowed by him after his death 'for three poor men and three poor women' of the parish. The two houses fulfilled this role until well into the 20th century, and were still benefitting from the interest on Tawney's bequest – including the dividends on his nine original £100 Oxford Canal Company shares – until at least 1922. Tawney's own house was next door, overlooking the brewery he operated with Mark and James Morrell, whose name it retained until its closure in 1998. The Tawney family had been successful river bargemasters, who moved into and married within Oxford's powerful brewing interests. By this means both Edward and his brother Richard (1721–1791), and their father Richard (1684–1756) before that, became prominent figures in the politics of the city in the 18th century. The only other building left on Lower and Middle Fisher Row after the 1954 clearances was The Nag's Head, traditionally *the* boating pub of Oxford.

The Nag's Head

Until the 1990s, there had been a pub called The Nag's Head on the corner of Hythe Bridge Street and Middle Fisher Row since at least the 1820s. Known in 1797 as The Fishes, when operated by an influential bargemaster called William Beesley (1754–1802), it was run by people with boating connections, including his descendants, well into the 20th century. The pub, which was known briefly as Navigation House in the 1870s, has always been at the centre of Oxford's social and commercial boating scene. In *The Flower of Gloster* (1911), after hiring a boat at the Basin, E. Temple Thurston records being told that The Nag's Head was the place to look 'if yer ever want a bargee in Oxford'. Consequently, once Thurston had explained his mission to engage a man and horse, 'the landlord brought in whisky and water to the little parlour of the Nag's Head, where … no doubt private transactions have taken place ever since the canals were opened'. All canal pubs had a role of this nature: people would look for work, buy and sell boats, horses, and equipment, exchange news, and leave or receive letters. The Nag's Head features in Evelyn Waugh's *Brideshead Revisited* (1945) as the pub frequented in 1923 by the

☞ Middle and Lower Fisher Rows are accessed by descending the steps by The Oxford Retreat which lead to the path alongside Castle Mill Stream. Care is needed when crossing Park End Street, beyond which is Lower Fisher Row, St George's Tower and the former Morrell's Brewery.

undergraduates Charles Ryder and Sebastian Flyte once they had 'formed the taste for lower company'. Waugh was writing from experience, having enjoyed the illicit thrill of drinking there himself as an undergraduate.

The present building was erected in 1939. Aubrey Tustin (Colin Tustin's grandfather) was the landlord before and after. Aubrey had married in 1909 Florence Corbey, from a boating family related to others including the Skinners, the Howkins, and the Bossoms. It was a sign of the declining importance of the boating clientele that no stables were retained when the new building went up, and that for the very first time the entrance was on Hythe Bridge Street rather than Middle Fisher Row. The pub was briefly renamed Antiquity Hall in the late 1990s (after another still older drinking establishment farther down Hythe Bridge Street, which had been demolished in 1869). This left local people to lament the loss of the familiar 'Nag's Head' name, and with it the meaningful associations with the tow-horses that were once so very important to almost everyone who downed a pint there. The pub is currently (2012) known as The Oxford Retreat.

Upper Fisher Row

To continue towards the Thames, cross Hythe Bridge Street by The Oxford Retreat and walk northwards along Upper Fisher Row immediately opposite.

Opposite The Nag's Head was another pub which celebrated its boating connections in its name. Like The Nag's Head, it had its own stables for use by tow-horses, and was run largely by families with boating connections. It had been known as The Racers and also The Race Horses in the 1820s and 1830s, but was known as The Running Horses from then on. It overlooked the site of the original ancient wharf, a spot known as 'Thieving Corner' from at least the 18th to the 20th centuries. The original building was pulled down in 1864, according to Henry Minn, and its replacement did not re-open after having been taken over by ARP (Air Raid Precautions) personnel in 1939.

A housing shortage after 1945 resulted in dozens of families living afloat in Oxford. One such was the James family, who lived on a converted narrowboat moored at the Hythe Bridge end of Upper Fisher Row. There were several children, contemporaries of Ray Titcomb and his sister, Della James. One of the boys, Jack, went on to help establish the Waterways Museum at Stoke

Bruerne on the Grand Union Canal in Northamptonshire. St Thomas' parish school occasionally played temporary host to children from visiting boats for a day or two even then. They were generally much envied, then and earlier. Through his friendship with Nancy Sherratt in the 1920s, for instance, Donald Willis often had occasion to visit the Basin, and recalled in his book *Early Days In Oxford*: 'It was always intriguing to watch the heavily laden barges towed into their off-loading berths by great shire horses, and I used to envy the sons of the bargees who, it seemed to me, lived gloriously interesting lives, eating and sleeping afloat – and, apparently, never going to school.'

The houses at the Hythe Bridge end of Upper Fisher Row were built in the late 1890s, in place of the 17th-century cottages which at one time lined the entire waterfront down to the Castle Mill. These cottages, and their predecessors, had been the homes of countless generations of boatmen's families, most of whom could claim centuries-old connections with the Row, some going back in all likelihood to the original colonies of fishermen. Mary Prior's meticulous research shows that most of the Row's old-established boating families – with names such as Beauchamp, Corbey, Crawford, Gardner, Howkins, and Skinner – had intermarried to a greater or lesser degree. This of course brought security to some, but put pressure on others. Almost from the moment that the Oxford Canal opened for business, two additional names stand out. The canal might have brought new opportunities for Fisher Row's closely knit community of boatmen, but for the Beesleys and the Bossoms in particular it also brought new frictions.

The Beesleys versus the Bossoms (see Appendix on page 99)

Although the family had been present in St Thomas' parish for many generations, the name Beesley was new to Fisher Row in 1789. Their arrival coincided with the completion of both the Oxford Canal and the Thames & Severn (T&S) Canal, which joined the Thames above Lechlade that same year, and made Oxford accessible from the Severn ports via Stroud. The Beesleys' arch business rivals for many decades to come would be a family with rather longer associations with both the Row and the river in general: the Bossoms. An early dispute occurred within a month of the completion of the Oxford Canal, *Jackson's* of 26 January 1790 noting a fight at Botley 'between two bargemen, Beasley and Bossom, over a difference on the river for a wager of 1 guinea'. The next year, *Jackson's* of 25 June reported a fight between Thomas Beesley and 'one of the crew of a Severn trow that had discharged her lading of salt, and was returned from London' to 'decide a dispute, and some trifling wager between themselves'. As the fight, held 'upon the little island above Folly Bridge', had already lasted an hour when a magistrate arrived, 'it was the general opinion that neither of them were sorry for this timely interference'!

The rivalry between the Bossoms and Beesleys continued largely unpublicised until 1822, when an unnamed Bossom was found guilty of destroying some 200 trees in the Beesleys' orchard to the north of Upper Fisher Row. In the interim, the Beesley brothers contented themselves with squabbling among themselves. Thomas Beesley (1768–1849) exploited the opportunities presented by the new T&S, a wide canal which – unlike the Oxford – was accessible to standard Thames barges. By 1795, he was the owner of seven barges capable of carrying 60 tons or more, making him the most important T&S bargemaster of the moment. Meanwhile, his older brother William (1754–1802), later the landlord of The Nag's Head, concentrated on the river trade between Oxford and London. The two brothers fell out mainly over the rights to onward movement of the cargoes arriving at the Oxford Canal terminus, on which William claimed a monopoly. Other members of the family and community were inevitably drawn into the feud. William was bound over to keep the peace in 1799 after assaulting a third brother, Samuel (1771–1841), who sided with Thomas, but, apparently undeterred, he was in the dock again a year later to answer for an assault on Thomas himself. The bargemen of St Thomas' were always reputed to be at the forefront of Oxford's regular 'town & gown' disturbances, and tales of violent confrontations among boatmen were commonplace, but this was probably just the natural way of things among men who lived physically demanding lives and were necessarily of a competitive character. (Jack Skinner could tell many a tale of bloody towpath duels, completely forgiven and forgotten over a pint the same evening.) However, the rift affected the social structure of the boating community: William's descendants tended to be connected with the canal, and resided in Middle Fisher Row, while Thomas' river allegiances were maintained in the Upper Row.

Members of the Beesley and Bossom families seem almost unassisted to have substantiated the popular opinion of the boating community as lawless, violent, immoral, and untrustworthy. Charles Bossom was an interesting example. Although there were two men of that name in St Thomas' parish at the time, it seems probable that it was the same individual who was publicly whipped for stealing ducks in 1754, acquitted of stealing corn from Folly Bridge wharf in 1758, and transported for seven years for stealing 'divers pieces of butcher's meat' in 1763. For some of Oxford's poorer 18th-century citizens, transportation was not always a bad thing. This certainly seems to have been true for Bossom, who had acquired a wife and family in Maryland by 1772, and was by then enjoying a happier existence in a land of relative plenty (see *Stories of Oxford Castle*). Extrapolating from Mary Prior's research (by her own admission, only tentative in respect of the Bossoms), it is possible that this Charles Bossom left a wife and three sons behind. If so, his was an important legacy, these sons being Thomas (1749–1834), William (1753–1813), and John (1762–?); the probable son of the latter, also named John (1802–75), was the first fully to establish the family's enduring association with Medley (see page 81).

The true extent of the bad blood between the two rival families can only be guessed, but the incidents which come through to us suggest all the ingredients of an epic historical soap opera, given substance with the realisation that the two families could in fact claim common descent. William Gardner (?–1705) was a boatmaster who was admitted a freeman of Oxford in 1674, and whose descendants married into both the Beesley and Bossom clans. The Gardners had been one of the dominant Upper Fisher Row families prior to the arrival of the canal in Oxford. It is probably due to them that the Upper Row became known as 'Pleasure-Boat Row'. It is only in a city like Oxford – with its never-ending supply of young undergraduates, with time and money on their hands – that the provision of boats for leisure use could be made viable, and when Henry Gardner (1724–1789), a nephew of William, died his residence was identified simply as Pleasure-Boat Row (as Upper Fisher Row continued to be known until at least the 1830s). But the Gardners were not simply in the business of hiring out rowing boats or punts. A 1784 notice in *Jackson's* advertised a raffle at Henry Gardner's premises, offering the chance to win for a guinea 'a very elegant pleasure boat with sash windows and blinds, two masts and flags, the stern end enclosed with neat iron rails, and several cupboards for provisions and liqueurs'. The luxurious indolence that this description conveys would be practically unthinkable on the canals for another two centuries.

It was the Beesleys who came to dominate the affairs of Upper Fisher Row, both numerically and commercially, through the younger of the two main feuding brothers, Thomas. He and his wife had 13 children between 1793 and 1817. One of his sons seems to have gone two better. *Jackson's* of 27 January 1838 thought it worth reporting that 'A poor woman of this city, wife of James Beesley, living in the Fisher-row, was a few days ago delivered of twins, making seven children in three confinements.' There is no record of the triplets in the baptism records of St Thomas' parish, but they do show that James' wife Elizabeth (née Hands) went on to have eight more children, including more twins in 1851. With so many mouths to feed, 'a poor woman' is how she was probably destined to stay, although by the end of the century two of her sons at least were running successful businesses: Geoffrey (1844–1909) would move out to Medley, where he rented out boats in competition with the Bossoms (see page 82); Jacob (1847–1929) remained on the Row, running the business first established by his father, James (1808–88). This was an osier works to the north of Upper Fisher Row, where the Beesleys' orchard had once been. It became well known, and a useful source of employment for local people. The osier is a small willow, which provides flexible shoots used mostly for items such as hampers, baskets, and creels (traps for fish, eels, and crayfish). In *Ramlin Rose*, Sheila Stewart quotes one boatwoman as saying it was '*cruel work. Women and children used to pull the rads* [reeds] *out of boilin' hot coppers and pull them through the stripping iron.*'

Meanwhile, the youngest of Thomas Beesley's 13 children, Samuel (1817–1901), found another way to maintain the family's traditional connections with the river: punt racing. This sport had been introduced as part of the annual Oxford Regatta in 1841. Inevitably the Beesleys and Bossoms were at the forefront, sustaining their simmering rivalry by treating the races, in the words of Mary Prior, as 'something between the duel, the joust, and the prize-fight'. Indeed, the races had to be suspended in 1845 owing to the excessive hostility of the competitors, and were only reintroduced in 1858, when Samuel Beesley dominated proceedings sufficiently to earn the nickname 'Sampson'. His nephew Abel Beesley (1851–1921), living in Middle Fisher Row, followed suit, becoming the national professional champion in 1878. When he retired undefeated in 1890 he was acknowledged as the sport's greatest ever exponent. Even after he had retired, Abel Beesley found plenty of opportunities to demonstrate his punting prowess. On one occasion at Maidenhead he defeated an opponent while using a billiard cue rather than a punt pole, and in 1910 he easily outpaced a steam-launch in a race from Medley to Godstow.

The last Beesley to live in the Row was Jacob's daughter, May. When she married one Frank Jones in 1915, this famous boating name was lost to the locality – although they had outlasted their rivals the Bossoms, who had long since moved out to Medley. The land by the lasher was sold for housing, the two semi-detached houses being the first Council houses in Oxford when built in 1919, according to Colin Tustin. Jones also sold off the long strip of land between the wall of Rewley Abbey and Castle Mill Stream. To the Tustins, this is known as the Flam – Oxford dialect for a low, watery, rushy place. During the Second World War, Ray Titcomb's father used to go out in a punt with Jones to scavenge for coal. It often spilled down to the water's edge where the railway locomotives refuelled to the north of the Sheepwash Channel. So many decades on from the arrival of that first boat from the Midlands, coal was still a commodity of paramount importance!

Rewley Abbey,
from James Ingram's
Memorials of Oxford,
1837.

Rewley Abbey and the Lasher

At the northern end of the Row is what is known as a lasher, an Oxfordshire term (as mentioned in relation to Wolvercote Lock) for a channel carrying surplus water away from a main watercourse, but more often, as here, for a sluice or weir by which the flow is controlled. The lasher appears to date from the 16th century – just one of many attempts over time to divert and control the water on which the rival mills of the Castle and Osney Abbey depended. It is here that the Oxford Canal Company culvert from Worcester College, source of the 1913 dispute between the College and the Company, empties into the Wareham Stream. Worcester College referred to it as Beesley's Lasher, a name dating back to 1795, when the influential Thomas Beesley took over the tenancy of the adjacent property.

To continue towards the Thames, take the path along The Flam between the Castle Mill Stream and an old stone wall, the only remnant of the 13th-century Cistercian abbey of Rewley. Midway along the wall is a 15th-century watergate, the sole feature of particular architectural interest. Once some 16 acres in extent, the Abbey's grounds included numerous streams, one of which is shown above, its course having been approximately where the stone wall ends. It was still apparent in the 1870s, but, like many of the Thames' rivulets and streams in Oxford ('more in number than your eyelashes', John Keats wrote in 1817), it has now disappeared.

Almost imperceptibly, the path leaves the Castle Mill Stream to follow the course of the Sheepwash Channel. This is a name of presumed antiquity, in view of its probable associations with the 'White Monks', as the Cistercians were called, on account of their woollen clothing and astute involvement in the woollen trade. The Abbey was dissolved in 1536.

Sheepwash Channel to Four Streams

Sheepwash Channel

For at least part of the 17th and 18th centuries, the Sheepwash Channel (sometimes incorrectly referred to as Rewley Abbey Stream) was part of a circuitous navigable route around Oxford, permitting vessels coming down the northern section of Castle Mill Stream from Medley to reach Oxford's other river wharf at Folly Bridge, via the Bulstake Stream around Osney. When Osney Lock opened in 1790, a more direct route from Medley was created, and seems to have made the Sheepwash briefly redundant. Certainly, that is the implication of a letter written on 12 April 1793 by the Reverend David Durell (1763–1852), the second of four generations of identically named Durells to hold a position of primacy within the Oxford Canal Company. At the time, with the Company contemplating the location of its new pound lock on to the Thames (see Isis Lock section), he described the Sheepwash as a stream 'not now in a navigable state but which might easily be rendered so'. He was right. Entries in the Thames Commissioners' ledgers between October and December 1796 record the expenses relating to 'Ballasting and Defining of the Sheepwash, a Chanel from the Cernal warff in to the Thames Navigation Oxford'. These were the words of John Treacher, who in 1791 became the first of three generations of Treachers to be appointed Surveyor of the entire Thames. Within Oxford, the family used wealth acquired as barge owners and brewers to become, much as the Tawneys did, influential in the local commerce and governance of Oxford. With the Sheepwash again open for navigation in 1796, Isis Lock

From Isis Lock (see page 48) the GWR bridge across Castle Mill Stream gives access to 'Snakes Island', and on towards the Thames.

was able to assume its enduring role as a pivotal structure of the Oxford waterway scene.

Where the Sheepwash and Castle Mill Stream meet is 'Snakes Island', as Ted Harris used to call it, a defiant reminder of the attractive mixed woodland which had established itself on the former coal yards and railway sidings prior to the construction of the housing of Rewley Park in the 1990s. Until then, the local name was still an appropriate one, with sightings of grass-snakes occurring here every summer – although the correct name for this large tract of land, extending all the way to Port Meadow, is Cripley Island. It is indicative of just how delicate the hydrology is here that the Sheepwash can flow in either direction, depending on the conditions.

The road bridge over the Sheepwash provides a view of a wonder of Victorian engineering, a swing bridge built by Robert Stephenson's engineers to allow the Buckinghamshire Railway (then London & North Western, later called the London, Midland, and Scottish, or LMS) to cross the Sheepwash to marshalling yards and a station on the site of the old Rewley Abbey. The first passenger train crossed in May 1851. A swing bridge was needed because it was impractical to build a fixed bridge here with the minimum ten-feet clearance required by statute over waterways used by the Oxford Canal Company. In about 1853, a locomotive toppled into the channel, the driver having failed to realise that the bridge had been opened for a boat to pass. Henry Taunt saw it being winched back to safety.

The LMS station closed for passenger traffic in October 1951, but goods trains continued to bring in domestic coal on a regular, if infrequent, basis. The default position of the bridge was as it is today, to allow boats to pass. Ray Titcomb, who often ventured this way from his childhood home in Upper Fisher Row, recalled that even when this was not the case, and the bridge stood across the Sheepwash, you could still wriggle underneath if clean clothes were not a priority! In 1975, the *Shell Book of Inland Waterways* assured the reader that 'if closed, application to the signalman or station staff will result in the appearance of a gang of spanner-men whose function is to unbolt the tracks prior to winding the span aside'. It was last operated for a rail movement in May 1984. For many decades, this astonishing example of Victorian ingenuity has remained a sadly neglected memorial to Oxford's disdain for its industrial heritage, but the future is more hopeful, with Oxford Preservation Trust now taking the lead in plans for its restoration.

Four Streams and Tumbling Bay

At the road bridge, the path leads back to Isis Lock in one direction and past the swing bridge and on towards the Thames in the other, passing beneath a railway bridge carrying the main Oxford to Birmingham line. It was built originally by the Oxford and Rugby Railway Co. in the 1840s. The junction of the Sheepwash with the Thames is known as Four Streams, the fourth of the crosswaters being the Bulstake Stream opposite. Four Streams is a name of some antiquity, going back at least to the mid-18th century, since it is named as such in *Jackson's* as early as 1757.

The ramp here is a reminder of the public ferry which once took passengers, including parties of schoolchildren from Jericho, across to the Tumbling Bay bathing area opposite. Its construction in 1853 ended for ever any prospect of the Bulstake Stream becoming again the important navigation artery that it had once been. River-fed bathing spots are not without their problems, however. A letter in the *Oxford Chronicle* of 6 July 1864 bemoaned the 'mud and weeds now almost meeting in the middle', notwithstanding the best efforts of 'our respected *merman* Thomas Beesley'. That name again, inseparable from things aquatic! And the attendant was still a Miss Beesley between the wars, according to Nancy Sherratt, who often used to walk here from her home in Hythe Bridge Wharf.

The fare for the ferry seems consistently to have been one penny. Nancy had vivid memories of the ferryman in the 1920s. Known as 'Butcher' Long, he was liked for his reassuring manner with those children who considered swimming an ordeal rather than a pleasure. One of the last men to hold the job seems to have been less considerate. He was an intimidating Cornishman called Archie, according to Charles Gee, whose family farm of Medley Manor extends all the way down to Tumbling Bay. The ferry was discontinued in 1955, and to reach Tumbling Bay now, a detour is required along the Botley Road. The term 'tumbling bay' was commonly used on the river in the 18th and 19th centuries to denote any outfall of water from a main watercourse, which is what the diminished Bulstake had indeed become. The name was also applied to the overflow channel near a lock.

At Four Streams a single-span footbridge carries the Thames Path over the Sheepwash towards Osney. This bridge was constructed in 1866, to replace an earlier wooden one which had three openings, according to a report on flood prevention made in 1877, and caused great inconvenience because of the sharp turn under it. This earlier bridge was presumably the one erected here by Daniel Harris of the Castle Gaol, and described by him in a letter-cum-report dated 29 January 1794 as being 'a bridge 50 feet long and Gates'.

Daniel Harris (c.1761–1840)

Harris' origins are obscure. A Thames Commissioners' report mentions in passing that he had been a journeyman carpenter on arrival in Oxford, and it is clear from his few surviving reports that he was not highly educated. This would make his rise to prominence in Oxford affairs all the more remarkable, since one gets the impression that despite his architectural and engineering skills, and eminent position at the prison, he was never quite taken seriously by his contemporaries. Thacker calls Harris' involvement with the locks at Osney and Godstow 'an occasion … for many public sarcasms' – the reason seeming to be the conceited derision of other, more professionally trained, engineers. Quite possibly his social class told against him: Thacker hints that he may have been from a long-established family of Thames fishermen called Harris living at Laleham in Surrey. Or perhaps his association with criminals was the problem. Whatever, the Thames Commissioners stuck with him, and entrusted him with repairing bridges and weirs, making gates, creating new channels and towpaths, and ballasting along a full 30 miles of river stretching from Rushey to Nuneham, work which is listed in full in his 1794 report.

On completion of this mammoth task, Harris seems to have done little further work on the river, but (as we have seen) found a continued demand for his services from the Oxford Canal

Company, with which his last recorded involvement came in 1804. In the 18 years since Harris had become prison governor in 1786, the waterway scene in Oxford had changed impressively for the better. A great deal of credit for this must go to Harris, who somehow also found time to illustrate the highly prestigious Oxford University Almanacs of 1789 to 1792, and in 1794 undertook extensive archaeological excavations of the prison premises, notably in relation to the Castle mound and crypt near St George's Tower. He also provided the illustrations for an account of the work, *Vestiges of Oxford Castle*. More about him appears in *The Abingdon Waterturnpike Murder* and *Stories of Oxford Castle*.

Harris married Elizabeth Tomkins, the daughter of a well-established High Street grocer, in 1789, and they had four daughters between 1791 and 1801. He remained Governor of the prison until 1809, then concentrated on commercial building projects until his death at his house in New Road in 1840.

 ## Four Streams to Binsey

The path from Four Streams to Godstow, where Harris supervised the construction of the pound lock begun in 1790, follows the eastern side of the river. The predecessor to this path, seemingly on the opposite side, owed much to Harris too. His 1794 account reveals the difficulties he faced in building structures able to withstand the challenging forces of the river: 'Opposite Fidlers Island and from thence to the Four Streams nearly, the towing path that was formed in the river, and that has been proved to stand, has been raised nearly half a yard and the work added to by stuff boated from near Osney.' When inspecting Harris' work in 1793, John Treacher had advised that the path needed to be repositioned on the opposite side, advice which was eventually followed to create the path we see today.

Strictly speaking the path is part of Fiddler's Island, separated from Cripley Island, the land immediately to the east, by a small stream called Fiddler's Stream. The earliest record of the name Cripley is in a lease of about 1138. The second syllable is probably derived – as too those of Osney, Medley, and Binsey (and even

To continue to Godstow from Four Streams, turn right and walk northwards with the river on your left. Or alternatively go left over the Sheepwash footbridge to find the Botley Road and Osney Lock.

Port Meadow, as in its original 'Portmaneit') – from the old English word for an island: 'eyot'. Substantial new buildings here constitute the loss of yet more of the river's natural flood plain, though the northern part of Cripley Island is still being utilised as allotments. These are visible where Fiddler's Stream first meets the towpath. 'Fiddler' is a name of considerable age, shown on Benjamin Cole's early 18th-century map of Port Meadow, but of uncertain origin.

Medley

At the northern end of Fiddler's Island, the old main Thames navigation of Castle Mill Stream flows eastwards on a course which then runs parallel to the canal southwards into the city. A little farther north, on the western bank of the Thames, lies Medley, for several centuries a favourite destination for boating parties from Oxford, and long before that a place of retirement and recreation for the monks of Osney Abbey, under whose jurisdiction all the land on the west side of the river lay. The Oxford historian Anthony Wood made frequent visits to Medley by boat in the mid-17th century, and Mrs Alicia D'Anvers, in *Humours of the University of Oxford*, called it in 1691:

> A place at which they never fail,
> Of custards, cyder, cakes and ale,
> Cream tarts and cheese cakes, good neats tongues
> And pretty girls to wait upon's.

George Wither (1588–1667), formerly of Magdalen College, had only one 'pretty girl' in mind in *A Love Sonnet*, which first appeared in print in 1620.

> In summer time to Medley
> My love and I would go.
> The boate-men there stood ready
> My love and I to row.
> For creame there would we call,
> For cakes, for pruines too.
> But now alas sh'as left me,
> Falero, lero, loo.

When Charles Gee bought Medley Manor Farm from Arthur Watts in 1957/8, Watts told him that the previous owner, Arthur Taylor, had earned the nickname 'Gooze-gog Taylor' on account of his reliably entertaining reaction whenever he discovered local boys pinching his gooseberry crop. Such activities were not always confined to boys, though, if the culprits apprehended in the act of stealing from Widow Taylor's Binsey orchard in 1781 are at all typical. For Thomas Pinnell, who drowned while attempting to escape, and an unnamed bargeman who assisted him, were both 'aged about eighty'!

Medley House

Successive 18th-century owners attempted to maintain Medley's reputation for leisure. Thomas Hearne noted in 1723 that 'Mr Swete is high-Sheriff this year for the County of Oxon ... He is a single man, and vastly rich. He hath an estate at Medley where he hath built a new house which shews him to be whimsical, the place being drown'd often in winter, and Medley being only a place of pleasure to go thither by boat in the summer season.' From the top of the house the view must have been quite sensational, looking across a largely treeless vista all the way to Worcester College and a backdrop of the city's famous spires.

In the 1760s Medley House was in the occupation of Thomas Potter, 'an eminent peruke [wig] maker'. Then came Francis Chillingworth, who announced, with a hint of desperation, in *Jackson's* of 2 May 1767 that he had 'taken and entered upon the Great House, and the Cheesecake House, at Medley' and that both would be 'commodiously fitted-up with all possible expedition; and where all those who are so obliging as to favour him with their company may depend on being accommodated with the best liquors of all kinds, tea, coffee, orgeat, cappilaire, cheescakes, custard etc etc, and where they may depend on civil treatment'.

'Civil treatment' and 'commodiously fitted-up' or not, the House was demolished in 1773. The auction notice in *Jackson's* of 13 June 1772 required that the purchaser remove all traces by Lady Day of the following year. Medley Manor Farm seems to have been built, or extended, almost adjacent at about the same time, making it likely that the stone was immediately incorporated

Medley House – 'a huge stone box with formal rows of flat windows', according to one contemporary commentator – was constructed around 1720 and demolished in 1773. It was 'much frequented in summer time by scholars, and others …', according to Thomas Hearne, '… it being wonderfull pleasant'. In the winter it was subject to regular flooding, and was a rather less attractive prospect!

into these farm buildings. The tradition of refreshment was maintained. When the farm and 80 acres of land came up for sale in 1790, the advertisement reveals that a Mr Wilkinson was running it as 'tea gardens' and that it was still 'a place of great resort'. The farm is now largely obscured by trees, but when it came on the market again in 1861, the owners continued to emphasise its leisure potential by advising that it was 'admirably adapted for the establishment of a place of public amusement, having a fine frontage to the River Isis and adjoining the boat lodges of Messrs Davis and Bossom so much frequented by members of the University'.

Bossom is a name as synonymous with Oxford's rivers as any, and boatbuilders of that name appear in the St Aldate's parish records from the end of the 17th century onwards. The Davis here referred to was Maximilian (1806–1879), whom the 1861 census records as being perhaps one of the first Oxford citizens officially to have resided on a boat, he and William Bossom (1838–1919) being 'house boat' neighbours at Medley that year. Maximilian was the brother of Stephen Davis (1799–1837), a boatbuilder at Folly Bridge whose importance in guiding rowing from a minor Oxford pastime to *the* pre-eminent University sport was considerable. Stephen Davis built the boat used in the very first Oxford–Cambridge boat race in 1829, and coached the winning Oxford crew, leading the *Sporting Magazine* of July 1829 to dub him 'the Professor of Rowing'. In November 1873, Maximilian's address was given in *Jackson's* as 'a house-boat on the River Isis'. As he had been swiftly summoned on the discovery of a drowned corpse in the Sheepwash Channel, it seems probable that his houseboat was located at this time at Tumbling Bay, where he was a bathing attendant at the time of his death. While Davis and Bossom are the first Medley boat-dwellers that can be positively identified, it is very likely that they were not the first: the description of John Day's premises in 1841 as 'Noah's Ark' would seem to tell its own story.

The Bossoms of Medley

The Bossom family comes to the fore again at Medley. But so too do the Beesleys, in perpetuation of the rivalries so prevalent in the story of Fisher Row. The Bossoms arrived first, it being in 1823, according to Thacker, that an otherwise unidentified William Bossom was noted as being in charge of 'Medley gates'. This is the weir which had been placed across the river by Samuel Simcock, the engineer who completed the Oxford Canal following the death in 1772 of his brother-in-law, James Brindley. In his 1794 report, Daniel Harris observed that Simcock had 'erected a stop lock as contracted for, similar to that erected by him at Kings Weir and has deepened for a considerable length above and thrown the stuff in order to form a towing path'.

John Bossom (1802–75) replaced William Bossom as keeper of Medley weir in 1838, and remained at least until 1867, according to Thacker. By 1871 the two houseboats of 1861 had grown to six. One, slightly apart, was still occupied by Maximilian Davis, 'proprietor of pleasure boats'; one by the erstwhile lock-keeper, John Bossom; two others by his sons, John (1828–1915) and William (1838–1919); and a fifth by his probable grandson, George (c.1848–?). Daring to place himself in the sixth was a Beesley, Geoffrey (1844–1909), who called himself an 'owner of boats' at this time, and a 'boatbuilder' in 1881. By 1891 he had moved off

Henry Taunt's photograph of about 1880 shows the rival firms of Bossom and Beesley at Medley. William Bossom's fleet is on the left; Geoffrey Beesley's on the right. In the foreground (right) is the houseboat of William's brother, 'the old veteran Charon' John, as Taunt called him.

Copyright: Oxfordshire County Council, Oxfordshire History Centre

the houseboat to live in Kingston Road, leaving Bossoms in sole occupancy of the three remaining boats.

Henry Minn recalled: 'From about 1880 to 1900 the Bossoms and Beasleys of Medley owned between them several hundred boats, and the river up to Godstow was crowded with them on a summer evening.' Henry Taunt corroborated this, writing in about 1900 that 'on both sides of the river, boats of all kinds including Centreboards, Sailing boats, Punts, Skiffs &c., are to be obtained from Geoffrey Beesley and the old veteran Charon John Bossom on the Port Meadow side, and from William Bossom on the towing path side'. In 1880 and 1881 the author, poet, and artist William Morris (1834–1896) took two trips along the Thames, to inform the writing of his futuristic 1890 novel *News from Nowhere*. On the first journey, he got to his home at Kelmscott from Medley 'in two pair-oared boats towed respectively by William Bossom and one of his men' as far as Newbridge, and from there 'muddled ourselves home somehow'.

A weir remained across both branches of the river at Medley until 1932, when dredging upstream produced enough depth for boats to move more certainly, and the weir became redundant. Until then, passage had been allowed only on two days of the

week, when the planks of the weir were abruptly withdrawn to allow boats to pass on a 'flash' of pent-up water. Henry Minn blamed the dredging for the demise of aquatic life in the river above Medley, but the partial removal of the flash weir in 1883 might have contributed too, since he recalled that 'up to about 1880 crayfish existed in great abundance and the local boatmen would take up a puntload of creels in the evening, drop them, and lift the following morning, often taking many hundreds in the night'. Before the southern section of the Meadow was raised by dumping city refuse here in the late 19th century, Minn says that the whole Meadow used to flood from about November to March, and that 'all the ditches around the Meadow were then quick running streams and swarming with crayfish'. These were the native white-clawed crayfish, now almost wiped out by the larger 'Signal' species introduced from north America.

Above Medley, the 'shallow water, swift running over a gravel bottom' formed 'one of the best short punting courses on the Thames', Minn recalled in about 1940. It 'swarmed with fish ... and I have seen old Jack Bossom with one throw of a cast net (now prohibited) catch more fish than would now be caught in a month's fishing'. The Jack Bossom referred to must be the same as the 'old veteran Charon' whom Taunt called John, and who died aged 86 in 1915. Minn recorded several encounters with him. In 1892 he photographed the Mayor's party beating the bounds of Oxford, the nature of which dictated that the journey would be made 'as far as possible by boat'. The occasion demanded many ritual toasts, one of which incorporated an obscure Oxford personage known as the King of the Slovens (or Sclavonians). Minn wrote: 'The King was always one of the oldest Freeman and a waterman. In 1892 the part was carried out by old Jack Bossom of Medley, one of the Univ. watermen, in a gaudy cloak and gilt cardboard crown.' Minn's other strong memory of Bossom, who remained living on his Medley houseboat into his eighties, was from the 1880s: 'He usually had his last dram at the Victoria Arms at the corner of St Johns Road and Walton Street, and at election time could always find his way home drunk, and shouting "Hall for ever!"' (A.W. Hall enjoyed an almost unbroken tenure as Oxford's Conservative MP from 1874 to 1892.)

Whereas in Fisher Row it was the Beesleys who saw off the Bossoms, at Medley it was the Bossoms who remained, albeit only until 1945, when the last of the family sold up. John Ballance, who purchased the business in 1953, honoured the family's long Medley presence by retaining the name, and had plenty of contact with the last of the Bossom family to retain riparian rights in Oxford. Tom Bossom operated as a river maintenance contractor, involving piledriving, dredging, and the like. 'Old Pa Bossom', John knew him as, *'the dearest old man you could ever wish to meet. You could mention any location on the river near Oxford, and he'd be able to tell you the exact nature of the bank, the bed, the depth – everything!'* Tom Bossom retired in the 1960s, ending at least 300 years of the family's direct association with the river. After the war, the main trade was still in the hiring of punts and rowing boats, but when virtually all of these were destroyed by fire in 1955, John and his partner, Derek Bennett, developed new technologies, including steam-powered vessels. One of the local people who worked for them was Alf Collins, whose father, William, had been the weir keeper at Medley from 1899 until his death in 1919. Collins, according to Thacker, was a long-established riverside name, known in many locations and over several generations, all along the river's course. William would have been the first occupant of the current Medley Weir Cottage, which was built in 1902 or 1903 to replace a smaller lock-keeper's house whose first occupant in about 1839 had been Jack Bossom's father, John. Alf died in 1990, and is buried in St Margaret's churchyard in Binsey, near his father, whose poverty denied him any marked grave.

At Medley there is an option to return to the Oxford Canal across Port Meadow. The Thames splits in two here. The bailey bridge across the eastern branch, the beginning of the Castle Mill Stream, was erected in 1947. An earlier wooden bridge had been destroyed when a floating workshop collided with it during the floods which followed the notoriously snowy winter of that year. A visiting company of Royal Engineers replaced it in a single Sunday afternoon the following September as a recruitment demonstration, watched by a large crowd. The way to Godstow takes us over the elegant 'rainbow' bridge. When

To return to the canal, turn right over the bailey bridge. Walton Well Road lies straight on across the Meadow, and Aristotle Lane diagonally to your left.

The Collins family outside Medley Weir Cottage, c.1914. William Collins was weir-keeper here from 1899 to 1919. He and his wife had six children, and those shown are probably Minnie, Percy, Nora, and Alf.

Picture courtesy of Tom Ballance; identifications by Peter and Heather Lund.

erected in 1865, it ended the age-old requirement either to ford the river here or use a ferry. A ford was obviously well established in 1731, when Christ Church requested that the City Council take down a gate and rails at Walton Ford on the opposite side of Port Meadow 'to make the passage clear for the tenants of Binsey to pass and repass with their carts and carriages'. The Botley Road did not become a reliable terrestrial route until the 1760s, and it is interesting to note that the Binsey ford was still in use – even in the winter – in 1825, as demonstrated by an account in *Jackson's* of the death of Elizabeth Bale of Godstow, whose drowned body was discovered as a team of horses was crossing the river, going either to or from Kidlington.

Queen's College Barge

Just upstream of Bossom's boat-yard lies the former Queen's College barge, one of the few remaining examples of the vessels which used to line the river below Folly Bridge. Before the construction of bankside boathouses, these barges were used as places for rowers to change, as well as to seat privileged spectators. The Queen's barge was built in 1903, and differs from those of the many colleges which had their barges built in the preceding 20 years, by having a steel rather than a wooden hull. It was also much less elegant than some, and one of the Fellows responsible for commissioning it later admitted to a 'struggle with my aesthetic conscience before approving the design'. John Ballance lived on the barge from 1953 to 1956, when it was moored near the bailey bridge. With economies all-important at this time, the temptation to sample a Port Meadow goose became just too great one cold Christmas Day. Aware that such opportunism might be frowned upon, he decided to destroy the evidence of the plucked feathers on the boat's stove. Minutes later, a snowstorm of goose down was swirling all around outside, propelled up the chimney and on to the roof in a very visual proclamation of John's guilt! Technically, the Port Meadow geese were the property of Wolvercote people and the owner of The Trout Inn at Godstow, and they used to be escorted daily to the river by goose boys or girls. The practice ceased at about this time, following the Second World War, with the result that some of the Wolvercote geese mated with wild stock, creating the hybrid 'Port Meadow Special' seen today.

Medley Sailing Club is the farthest upstream of all the Thames sailing clubs. It had its origins in the 1930s, but was not established in any formal sense until 1947. Fred Hann, the Juxon Street wharfinger, was one of its founder members. The club moved a short distance to its present site in 1959.

 ## Binsey to Godstow

To reach Binsey, turn left along the rough track to the north of Medley Sailing Club, then right at the end. Or continue along the river path towards Godstow (turn to page 90).

Beyond the Sailing Club, the walker has the option of a detour to Binsey village and St Margaret's Church. In 1837 James Ingram noted of Binsey in *Memorials of Oxford*: 'In 1771 there were only twelve houses in the parish, and they have not increased much since.' Even now, nothing much has changed!

The Perch Inn

Of these dozen or so buildings, there is most to say about The Perch. Parts of the building date from the 17th century, contemporary with the earliest identifiable licensee of a Binsey alehouse. This was Thomas Prickett, in April 1651. The Pricketts are a family with as old an association with the village as any: even in 1598 a Robert Pricket had maintained that his family had resided there 'since time out of mind'. The family continued to run the pub until 1761, when Margaret Prickett, as the widow of Robert Tawney (1679–1745), was succeeded by her son, Thomas Tawney. One of the Tawneys' customers must have been the New College scholar James Woodforde (1740–1803), who made several excursions with friends 'up the water' to 'Binzy for victuals and drink' in the 1760s. Invariably they took the opportunity to play 'skettles', an activity that the University would have frowned upon. The understanding was that the loser would pay for the hire of their boat.

Binsey's unusual extra-parochial status – falling within the jurisdiction of the city of Oxford, yet remote from it, and physically on the Berkshire side of the Thames – has given it a certain historical notoriety, and while there is nothing especially unusual about the bloodthirsty Whit-Monday entertainment advertised on a handbill of about 1814 – 'two capital bulls will be brought to the stake, and, for the greater entertainment of the company … a good fresh badger will be baited' – the staking of the bulls is interesting in suggesting an activity which may have been traditional enough to inspire the naming of the nearby Bulstake Stream. Henry Taunt tells us that later in the century The Perch was dubbed 'Binsey Cathedral' because the landlord was not averse to ignoring the constraints of Sunday licensing laws.

In 1830, the leaseholder of a sizeable Binsey agricultural estate which included the 'well-accustomed' public house, called at this time The Fish, was Richard Gee (of no known relationship to the current proprietors of Medley Manor Farm). When Richard died in 1842, and the estate was put up for sale again, the pub was referred to for the first time as The Perch. In the mid-1870s, the publican was Henry Goatley (c.1847–?), who described himself as both a boatbuilder and a victualler, but by 1881 had moved on to a houseboat at Medley. A neighbour, also a boatbuilder, was his brother Thomas (c.1842–?), who in 1874 married a local girl, Mahalah Howse. Howse is a very significant name, one John Howse (c.1534–?), back in 1583, having been the very first Oxford 'boteman' to become a freeman of the city. This established the fundamental importance of the occupation, and set the foundations for families like the Tawneys and Treachers subsequently to become such powerful establishment figures. George Goatley, the son of Thomas, ran The Perch from at least 1911 to 1935. Heather Lund, a resident of Binsey for 50 years, said that Goatley had often provided the impoverished Collins children (who had been unceremoniously evicted with their mother from Medley Weir Cottage on the death of their father in 1919) with badly needed porridge for breakfast.

C.S. Lewis made his first visit to Binsey around the same time, cycling there on 'a gloomy and fogged day' in November 1922. Responding to Lewis' desire to visit some 'melancholy place which would underline the mood of the day', a friend had taken him to what Lewis called 'a sad church by a woodside'.

St Margaret's Church

To reach St Margaret's Church, take the lane which turns sharply right beyond the row of cottages.

Most English villages cluster round their pub and church. Binsey is different, in that it has had to choose between the two. The pub has won this contest. Binsey's church lies half a mile away to the north-west. It is a longish detour from the towpath of this book's title (and walkers should allow a return time of about an hour), but it has sufficient connections with the river to justify inclusion, and is in any case a supremely atmospheric place in which to take a few moments' rest.

The church, with only a farmhouse for company, stands at the end of a lane which was first laid out in 1821. When Althea Prickett (1880–1973) moved out of the farm in 1956 (shortly before John Ballance moved in), the ancient connection of the Pricketts with this location was broken. In conversations with Heather Lund, Althea claimed that the Pricketts had resided there since Saxon times, when the site was known (as recorded in the Domesday Book) as Thornbiri.

When Thomas Hearne visited the church in December 1718, as well as chatting to Thomas Prickett (c.1658–1738?), who had been the sole churchwarden for 38 years, he found the grave of Jeffrey Ammon, who had 'desired to be buried here, because he us'd often to shoot hereabouts Snipes … & other Things'. Ammon, whom Hearne had known as the landlord of Antiquity Hall in Hythe Bridge Street, had 'desired a certain friend (viz. Will Gardner, a boatman of Oxford who used to rowe him) to put now and then a bottle of ale by his grave when he came that way, which accordingly he has done'. The common descent of the Beesleys and the Bossoms from the Gardners has already been referred to, and by extrapolating from Mary Prior's family trees, it would appear that this Will Gardner's father, William (?–1705), is the man from whom the two lines derived (see Appendix). Hearne's chance remembrance of the name adds historical context to an otherwise inconsequential, if droll, diary entry.

Hearne also noted 'an old Well on the West Side of Binsey Church, which … hath been very famous in the Popish Times'. Indeed it had, for it was St Frideswide, Oxford's patron saint, who is supposed to have summoned the spring here, while fleeing the unwanted attentions of a royal suitor at the turn of the 7th and 8th centuries. One variant of the tale tells how Frideswide fled to Binsey by boat, and used the spring water to restore the sight of the blind swineherd who had given her shelter. Who knows, if the Prickett tradition of Saxon lineage is correct, the patient might even have been one of their forebears! The fame of the well became widespread in mediaeval times and attracted huge numbers of pilgrims. It is this well which Lewis Carroll incorporated into *Alice's Adventures in Wonderland* as the 'treacle well' that the Dormouse describes at the Mad Tea-Party; formerly 'treacle' had the meaning of 'medicine'. The Thames was a fundamental influence on the creation of the 'Alice' stories, and Godstow is particularly important as the place where The whole process began on a boat outing on 4 July 1862. (This subject is considered in detail in *Alice in Waterland*.)

The Tawney family's connections with The Perch have already been referred to, and when one of the most eminent, the wealthy brewer and magistrate Richard, died in 1756, *Jackson's* recorded on 28 February:

> The Gentlemen of this Corporation attended his funeral in their formalities, when his corpse was carried up the water, according to his own directions, and interred with his ancestors at Binsey, on which occasion such a prodigious concourse of people attended to pay this last tribute of friendship, that there were many hundreds more than the church could contain.

Richard was the brother of Robert, the Binsey publican who married Margaret Prickett in 1710. Two other important members of the Tawney family are buried at St Margaret's Church: Richard's sons, Edward (1735–1800) and Sir Richard (1721–91), both of whom we have encountered before. Both served three times as Oxford's Mayor, and it is Edward's benefaction which paid for the Tawneys' memorial inside the church.

'First the church and then The Perch!' was once a Binsey saying. The phrase can be taken in two ways. It might reflect the greater antiquity of the original Saxon church, or, more likely, the customary Sabbath-day order of things: first pay your respects to the Lord, then your pennies to the landlord! As The Perch is almost unavoidable when returning from the church to the river, you may wish to repeat this time-honoured ritual! (Indeed, it will save considerable time to schedule your visit during opening hours, in order to take the short-cut back to the river through the pub's garden.)

Port Meadow

To rejoin the river bank from St Margaret's Church, a return journey is required back through Binsey village. During opening hours the towpath can be accessed via the garden of The Perch Inn.

A little to the north of The Perch is the place where the second of Binsey's three fords once lay. Fred Thacker, writing in 1920, asserted that the ford 'crossed at the single withy tree on the towpath about a hundred yards above the south end of Binsey Green'. Tom Ballance remembered playing by the stump of an old tree here as a child in the 1950s, and also recalled the relative shallowness of the river at that point. A little farther on and the river bends to the west at Black Jack's Hole, a name which alludes to the very deep water found here in the past. It was a spot well known for its especially large pike, and according to Henry Taunt parents deterred their children from bathing there with a tale of how 'the hole was tenanted by a horrid black sprite, who did his best to detain anyone trenching on his part of the stream, and that he even objected to fish being angled for in his domain'. Black Jack's Hole was also known as a suicide spot, one reason perhaps why the Oxford University Humane Society chose to locate their house-boat there in Taunt's time, so that its members, 'with the initials of the society on their caps', could be readily available if the need arose.

Above Black Jack's Hole there was once a third crossing point, known as Peel Yat Ford. This traditional assertion by the freemen of Oxford was corroborated, according to Minn, in 1927, when the stones which formed the paved approach to the crossing were dredged up. Here too is a line of rare native black poplars, planted by the Oxford Civic Society to replace those felled for railway use in the mid-19th century, and lamented in Gerard Manley Hopkins' moving 1879 poem, 'Binsey Poplars'.

From any convenient spot on the bank here, the sheer grandeur of Port Meadow is amply displayed, and it is easy to see why the place has been a favourite with horseriders for so very long. For 200 years between 1680 and 1880 it played host to Oxford's famed annual horse races – but had no doubt seen many similar such gatherings ever since it was bequeathed to the city by a grateful King Alfred (so the story goes) in the 9th century. The race course lay towards the northern end of the Meadow. The river provided convenient drinking water for the horses, but had other uses too. *Jackson's* reported with some satisfaction in 1764 that 'a fellow in trowzers, meanly drest, was detected in picking a gentleman's pocket near the stand; upon which he was immediately conducted to the river, and severely disciplined'. But sometimes the river was the salvation of wrong-doers too! Henry Minn recorded: 'one of my distinct recollections as a child is seeing a "Welsher" at the Races escape from the angry crowd by wading the river from the Meadow to the towing path.' After a gap of exactly a century, the Port Meadow horse races were resumed in 1980, but, unable nowadays to rely on the patronage of the aristocracy as in days gone by, they have again been discontinued. All traces of the original course were lost when the Meadow was used as an aerodrome during the 1914/18 war.

Numerous less celebrated contests have also occurred on Port Meadow. Take the race between 'a broken-winded poney' and 'a blind gelding' belonging to Mr Bull and Mr Heynes, and run over 10 miles for a wager of 100 guineas in 1774. Humans too have pushed themselves to the limit. There was a journeyman carpenter who was challenged to run 50 miles in ten hours in 1787, for instance, and an unnamed man who, 'before a great concourse of people', undertook to throw a stone a distance of 180 yards for a wager of £40 in 1799; and then there was James Jones, who was set the 'task of walking 1050 miles in 20 successive days on the race course' in 1817. All three men succeeded, incidentally, and it was Mr Heynes' blind gelding that won in 1774, in case you were wondering!

The Meadow has long been a favourite location for other kinds of sport too. It is perhaps not surprising to find the Oxford Cricket Club playing matches here as early as 1762, since the game first developed in public schools. In 1760 James Woodforde played in matches made up entirely of scholars who had attended Winchester and Eton, and it was 'school professionals' of this kind who consistently represented Oxford against Cambridge, once the fixture commenced in 1827. In the 1870s Kenneth Grahame, crossing the canal from St Edward's School, enjoyed the liberating lack of boundaries which meant that 'if an ambitious and powerful slogger wanted to hit a ball as far as Wolvercote, he could do so if he liked'.

In winter, the place has always been ideal for skating. Its propensity to flooding, combined with generally more severe winters, made skating an obvious joy – and not only among the general public. By the early 19th century, skating was becoming a recognised sport, inspiring *Jackson's* to record in January 1838:

> Skaiting, it appears, has become a complete science, and it was particularly exemplified during the last week in Port Meadow. Many scientific skaiters exhibited their various degrees of skill, but the extraordinary performances of Mr Arthur Tyror, of this city, excited the attention and astonishment of every one who saw him. He is probably the best skaiter in the country, and his introduction of a set of skaiting quadrilles gave great satisfaction to a numerous assemblage of persons.

Two more items from *Jackson's* give a glimpse of a rather different seasonal pastime. The offer of a reward for a lost dog in 1766 reveals that her master was engaged in 'swallow-shooting', and a report of the death of a Hythe Bridge waterman, Edward Crawford, in 1786 revealed that he had 'taken some gentlemen up the river, and landed them in Port Meadow to shoot swallows'. Swallows were not the only thing shot on Port Meadow. In 1774, an inquest into the death of a labourer called James Glassington found he had been shot by all three of the other passengers on the boat they had taken from Medley to the city – although only one of them, James Smith, the last to fire, was found guilty.

Whatever their intentions, Oxford's citizens are lucky indeed to have the great expanse of the Meadow so conveniently close to hand. Even in less populous times, it was appreciated in much the same way as now. Samuel Ireland's sentiments, recorded in *Picturesque Views on the River Thames* (1792), would be shared by many still today:

> The beauty of the scenery a little below Godstow still increases, and the river, nobly expanding itself, seems proudly urging its courses to pay its tribute to that ancient and noble seminary of learning, Oxford, whose venerable towers and lofty domes all happily unite to form a general mass of objects superior to any thing which the country can boast.

With the proliferation of new canalside housing on the far side, the view (especially in winter) may no longer be matchless, but Port Meadow *is* still a sensational place: always surprising, always evocative, and always providing a sense of space, freedom, and natural harmony. But as urban Oxford creeps ever closer, the plea of *The Spectator* in 1914 is as pertinent today as it was then:

> Hitherto it has resisted all sophistication, and refuses to be turned into a city park with ordered drives and flower-beds and policemen. From Walton Well to Wolvercot it still stretches, a wilderness of green turf, the joy of the rider and walker, and the airiest meadow in the valley of the Thames. So be it, and so shall it be.

Godstow Lock

Construction began on the first pound lock at Godstow in 1790. The prison governor Daniel Harris supervised the work, causing the 'many public sarcasms' noted by Thacker. At the same time, an artificial cut was dug to take the river under a new bridge down to the lock. When Samuel Ireland passed this way in 1791 he noted that 'the cut is now forming'; by 1794, it had been finished, enabling William Combe to avoid the 'pretty strong current … and inconvenient bend' of the former channel flowing past The Trout Inn. The excavation of the new channel through the grounds of Godstow Nunnery disturbed many stone coffins and skeletons. More were discovered in 1885, when the river was widened, and coffins have continued to appear within living memory. Prior to 1885, according to Minn, 'the stream was so silted and grown up with weeds a boat always had to be towed'. This is corroborated by the 1877 Royal Commission into flood prevention on the Thames, which observed that although the lock had been rebuilt in 1876, the stream was still too shallow and clogged for use. The lock had a major refurbishment after the First World War, and reopened in May 1924.

Godstow Nunnery

Founded in about 1133, the Nunnery's most famous novice was Rosamund Clifford, who became the youthful mistress of Henry II. Raphael Holinshead, writing in the 16th century, celebrated her 'beauty, properness of person, and pleasing wit, with other amiable qualities', attributes which earned 'Rosamund the Fair' enduring popular affection. Some six centuries after her burial at the Nunnery in about 1176, these two verses from a long poem were published in *Jackson's* when a hurricane caused severe damage in January 1764:

> Loos'd by the wintry Wind and driving Rain,
> Here Stones disjointed seem to hang in Air;
> Fall'n is the Gate, which ne'er shall close again,
> No more the Prison of the cloister'd Fair.

> The Heiffer plucks the Ivy from the Wall
> Fall'n, Godstow, is the Glory of thy Dome!
> Weep, Stranger, as thou passest, weep at its Fall,
> And strew a Flow'r on Rosomonda's Tomb.

Not everyone was so reverential. The Bishop of Lincoln had ordered her reburial 'without the church' in order that 'other women, warned by her example, may refrain from unlawful and adulterous love', and both Samuel Ireland and William Combe, visiting in the 1790s, noted this Latin inscription on a wall, presumed to be a recent 'quibble' inspired by John Leland's

16th-century assertion that when her coffin was opened 'a sweet smell came out of it':

> Here Rose the graced, not Rose the chaste, reposes,
> The smell that rises is no smell of roses.

After dissolution, the Nunnery became the residence of Henry VIII's doctor, George Owen (who at the same time acquired the extensive meadowland on which Jericho would be built some three centuries later). Parts were destroyed during the Civil War, after which it became more and more dilapidated. However, even as a ruin, Godstow, 'God's Place', remained inspirational, and Samuel Ireland's 1792 description still rings true today:

> the Gothic simplicity and the antiquity of Godstow bridge with the adjoining remains of the nunnery wall, and contiguous woody scenery, the perpetual moving picture on the water produced by the passage of west country barges, and the gayer scenes presented by the pleasure boats and select parties from the neighbouring university, render it in every point of view a happy subject for the pencil.

'View of Godstow Nunnery near Oxford' from *England Displayed* (1769) seen before the artificial cut (the main course of the river today) was made through the graveyard. The tower in the centre seems to show signs of the damage caused by the hurricane of a few years earlier. The chapel on the right is still discernible today. Godstow House (The Trout) stands at the far end of the footbridge over the river's original course.

The Trout Inn (Godstow House)

Another 'happy subject for the pencil' is The Trout, formerly known as Godstow House, positioned by one of the key bridges across the Thames on what was the river's main course before the construction of Godstow Lock. The original building probably

Leave Port
Meadow
through the
gate to the
north of the
Nunnery. The
entrance to
The Trout is
on your right.

replaced the cottage of a fish-weir keeper. Anthony Wood visited this 'Godstow alehouse' in the 1660s and 1670s. In 1737 it was almost entirely rebuilt by Jeremiah Bishop, or 'Old Jerry' as he was known. When he died at the age of 85 in 1771, his obituary noted that he had run the place for 60 years, and 'was well-known to most of the Gentlemen who have been members of the University within the last fifty years'. The Bishop family also oversaw Godstow Lock in its early years. It was a peculiarity of the lease that, at least until the early 1900s, the lock-keeper was prohibited from selling any kind of refreshment, to ensure maximum business for the pub.

When beating the bounds of the city franchise, it was usual for the Mayor's party to stop at Godstow House for dinner and refreshments. Henry Minn went along in 1892, and noted this from the 1800 account by which they were guided: 'Disembarking at Godstow House go through the House. It is remarkable that altho the Magistrates of Oxford grant the licence to this House they cannot take cognizance of disorderly behaviour amongst the customers, the tap-room and kitchen as well as the cellar being without the franchise of the City.' It may have been members of the Mayor's retinue who were themselves guilty of 'disorderly behaviour' in 1860. J.R. Green noted that when the party continued across Port Meadow, 'as the plankbearers had got too drunk to stir, the mayor had to jump ditches, *idem* the mace'. Apparently undeterred, however, he 'did wonders and reflected credit on the city'.

Minn recalled that from 1880 onwards boating was 'one of the chief amusements of Oxford youth, and the Trout a favourite resort. The Bossoms and the Beesleys at Medley had at this period several hundred boats between them, and a large number of these would be found at the Trout on fine summer evenings.' At that time the inn, which had adopted the name of The Trout by the 1840s, was kept by Mrs Arabella Mumby. She had succeeded her parents (William and Georgiana Lipscombe, who had run the pub since the 1830s). Arabella was one of seven sisters. They evidently had something in common with 'Rosamund the Fair'. The young William Morris did not hesitate when encouraged by Dante Gabriel Rossetti to attempt (albeit unsuccessfully) to persuade the Lipscombes' 18-year-old 'stunner' of a daughter (presumably Georgiana, the youngest) to sit for him in 1857, and over 20 years later the memory of the sisters' allure remained strong. On the 1880 trip already referred to, when being towed by William Bossom, Morris and his friends made a special point to 'hove to just above Godstow Lock … in order to revisit the home of the four Miss Lipscombs'.

The Trout lost Minn's custom in November 1897, when it was converted in a way which 'destroyed the old lonely character of the house by adopting the methods and style of a Birmingham hotel'. He may not have returned for some time: *Punch* was still lamenting its continued modernisation in 1922. A long poem ends with the lines:

> Here is the crowning crime and scandal
> That such an honest English inn
> Should fall before the 'cultured' vandal.

Today The Trout has regained a good measure of its centuries-old charm and popularity. On a busy day, it is difficult to imagine what a lonely spot this must have been in times past, at a critical entry point into the Liberties of the City of Oxford. Yet come here in winter, let the passing Thames influence your perception, and the words of The Trout's own leaflet from the late 1950s do indeed seem apt still: 'an old, grey, stone, riverside building, blended quietly into the background, as natural and harmonious as if it had been planted and grown there … a haven, a deep-rooted symbol of peace and permanence in these hurried and bewildering times'.

The Trout lies nearly a mile away from the Oxford Canal, which is reached by following the main Godstow Road through Lower Wolvercote. On the way you will cross the stream which once fed the Wolvercote Paper Mill, which Thomas Combe had purchased in 1855. Combe was a patron of, among other Pre-Raphaelite artists, William Holman Hunt, who in the 1850s liked to make 'the fields of Godstow my studio until sunset'. He would then meet up with the Combes and others at the Mill to make 'a pleasant party with whom to return by twilight' to Jericho.

Lower Wolvercote boasts two old pubs, The Red Lion and The White Hart. Perhaps it was over-indulgence at one of these hostelries which caused the extraordinary behaviour of one of the Beesley clan in 1829. The facts of the case, as reported in *Jackson's*,

To reach the canal, go as far as the steps which lead down to Wolvercote Lock on the left-hand side of the road, just after it crosses the railway. Alternatively, frequent buses run from Wolvercote to Oxford.

were that Thomas Beesley (1801–?) was accused of stealing a duck from the common Wolvercote stock on Port Meadow. Just as Beesley was denying it, 'the duck quacked; it was in his pocket'! Beesley was the grandson of William, the oldest of the quarrelsome Beesley brothers of Fisher Row, and seems to have inherited his grandfather's pugnacity. A fight ensued, which was resumed the same evening, when Beesley and some accomplices 'again went into Port Meadow, and proceeded to vent their fury on the cattle and poultry'. The intruders then moved to stand provocatively on the canal bridge near The Plough. In the ensuing fracas a 16-year-old called John Barrett was fatally wounded when Beesley 'without the slightest provocation, struck him a terrific blow on his head with a bludgeon, which felled him to the ground, and from which he was removed weltering in blood, and totally insensible'. Beesley then fled, rescued by some friends in a boat. As a consequence we have a rare description of a member of this prolific family:

> about 30 years of age, about 5 feet 7 inches in height, middle sized, light complexion, rather freckled face, rather dark hair, whiskers a little sandy, has the appearance of a boatman or bargeman, had on a pair of fustian trowsers, red plush waistcoat, with brown fustian sleeves, and a pair of half-boots, a black leather cap, bound round with fur; walks rather stiffly with one leg.

Beesley was soon apprehended, and sentenced to fourteen years' transportation for manslaughter, although he actually served his sentence aboard a prison hulk only until 1839, then returned to live back at Fisher Row.

Not just water under the bridge

This unsavoury brawl has taken us from the river margins back to the Oxford Canal. The Thames is most notable for its picturesque views and changing moods; the canal for the stirring story of its survival. Both waterways are testimonies to the many individuals who have shaped the precious and vibrant 'living heritage' that we see today. If this book has helped in any small way to further the appreciation of that heritage, and the importance of its conservation, it will have fulfilled its role.

select genealogy of Oxford boating families

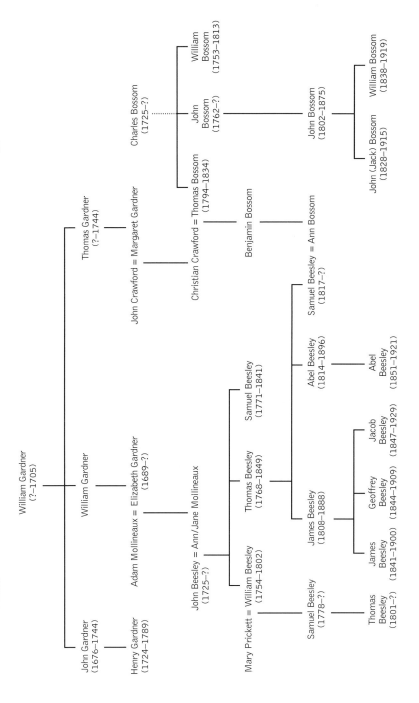

This genealogy is based on the research of Mary Prior.

Sources and further reading

Kingsley Belsten: various articles for *The Oxford Times*, 1964–1971

Hugh J. Compton: *The Oxford Canal* (David & Charles, 1976)

Mark J. Davies: *The Abingdon Waterturnpike Murder* (Oxford Towpath Press, 2008)
— *Stories of Oxford Castle: from Dungeon to Dunghill* (Oxford Towpath Press, 2006)
— *Alice in Waterland: Lewis Carroll and the River Thames in Oxford*
   (Signal Books, 2012)

C. and E. Hibbert (eds.): *The Encyclopaedia of Oxford* (Macmillan, 1988)

Herbert Hurst: *Oxford Topography* (Clarendon Press, 1899)

Oxford Archaeology: *Castle, Canal & College* – Historic Context Study and
   Conservation Plan (2008)

Mary Prior: *Fisher Row: Fishermen, Bargemen and Canal Boatmen 1500–1900*
   (Clarendon Press, 1982)

Catherine Robinson and Elspeth Buxton: *Hayfield Road: Nine Hundred Years
   of an Oxford Neighbourhood* (1993)

Catherine Robinson and Liz Wade: *A Corner of North Oxford: The Community
   at the Crossroads* (2010)

Thomas Squires (ed.): *In West Oxford: Historical Notes and Pictures Concerning
   the Parish of St Thomas the Martyr* (Mowbray, 1928)

Sheila Stewart: *Ramlin Rose: The Boatwoman's Story* (Oxford University Press, 1993)

Henry W. Taunt: *Godstow … Medley, Whytham, & Binsey* (Taunt & Co, c.1900)

Fred S. Thacker: *The Thames Highway, Volumes I and II* (1914 and 1920, reprinted
   by David & Charles in 1968)

The Victoria History of the County of Oxfordshire, Volume IV (Oxford University
   Press, 1979)

Liz Woolley: *Oxford's Working Past* (Huxley Scientific Press, 2012)

Index